PYTHON NUMPY BEGINNERS

NUMPY SPECIALIZATION
FOR DATA SCIENTISTS

AI PUBLISHING

First Printing, 2021

Edited by AI Publishing
eBook Converted and Cover by AI Publishing Studio
Published by AI Publishing LLC

ISBN-13: 978-1-956591-09-5

How to Contact Us

If you have any feedback, please let us know
by emailing contact@aipublishing.io.

Your feedback is immensely valued,
and we look forward to hearing from you.
It will be beneficial for us to improve
the quality of our books.

To get the Python codes and materials used in this book,
please click the link below:

www.aipublishing.io/book-Numpy-python

The order number is required.

About the Publisher

At AI Publishing Company, we have established an international learning platform specifically for young students, beginners, small enterprises, startups, and managers who are new to data science and artificial intelligence.

Through our interactive, coherent, and practical books and courses, we help beginners learn skills that are crucial to developing AI and data science projects.

Our courses and books range from basic introduction courses to language programming and data science to advanced courses for machine learning, deep learning, computer vision, big data, and much more, using programming languages like Python, R, and some data science and AI software.

AI Publishing's core focus is to enable our learners to create and try proactive solutions for digital problems by leveraging the power of AI and data science to the maximum extent.

Moreover, we offer specialized assistance in the form of our free online content and eBooks, providing up-to-date and useful insight into AI practices and data science subjects, along with eliminating the doubts and misconceptions about AI and programming.

Our experts have cautiously developed our online courses and kept them concise, short, and comprehensive so that you can understand everything clearly and effectively and start practicing the applications right away.

We also offer consultancy and corporate training in AI and data science for enterprises so that their staff can navigate through the workflow efficiently.

With AI Publishing, you can always stay closer to the innovative world of AI and data science.

If you are eager to learn the A to Z of AI and data science but have no clue where to start, AI Publishing is the finest place to go.

Please contact us by email at
contact@aipublishing.io.

AI Publishing Is Searching for Authors Like You

Interested in becoming an author for AI Publishing?
Please contact us at author@aipublishing.io.

We are working with developers and AI tech professionals just like you to help them share their insights with global AI and Data Science lovers. You can share all your knowledge about hot topics in AI and Data Science.

Table of Contents

Preface

With the rise of data science and high-performance computing hardware, programming languages have evolved as well. Various libraries in different programming languages have been developed that provide a layer of abstraction over complex data science tasks. Python programming language has taken the lead in this regard. More than 50 percent of all data science-related projects are being developed using Python programming.

If you ask a data science expert what the two most common and widely used Python libraries for data science are, the answer would almost invariably be the NumPy library and the Pandas library. And this is what the focus of this book is. It introduces you to the NumPy and Pandas libraries with the help of different use cases and examples.

Thank you for your decision to purchase this book. I can assure you that you will not regret your decision.

§ Book Approach

The book follows a very simple approach. The 1st chapter is introductory and provides information about setting up the installation environment. The 1st chapter also contains a brief crash course on Python, which you can skip if you are already familiar with Python.

The rest of the book contain five chapters. Chapter 2 provides a brief introduction to the NumPy array. You will study how to create NumPy arrays and add, remove, and print items in NumPy arrays. Chapter 3 focuses on NumPy arrays manipulation concepts such as sorting, reshaping, and indexing. Chapter 4 provides miscellaneous tips and tricks for the NumPy library. The 5th chapter explains how you can perform mathematical operations with NumPy, while the 6th chapter explains the process of creating an artificial neural network with NumPy from scratch.

Each chapter explains the concepts theoretically, followed by practical examples. Each chapter also contains exercises that students can use to evaluate their understanding of the concepts explained in the chapter. The Python notebook for each chapter is provided in the *Codes Folder* that accompanies this book. It is advised that instead of copying the code from the book, you write the code yourself, and in case of an error, you match your code with the corresponding Python notebook, find and then correct the error. The datasets used in this book are either downloaded at runtime or are available in the *Resources* folder.

Do not copy and paste the code from the PDF notebook or Kindle version, as you might face an indentation issue. However, if you have to copy some code, copy it from the Python Notebooks.

§ Who Is This Book For?

The book is aimed ideally at absolute beginners to data science in specific and Python programming in general. If you are a beginner-level data scientist, you can use this book as a first introduction to NumPy. If you are already familiar with Python and data science, you can also use this book for general reference to perform common tasks with NumPy.

Since this book is aimed at absolute beginners, the only prerequisites to efficiently use this book are access to a computer with the internet and basic knowledge of programming. All the codes and datasets have been provided. However, you will need the internet to download the data preparation libraries.

§ How to Use This Book?

In each chapter, try to understand the usage of a specific concept first and then execute the example code. I would again stress that rather than copying and pasting code, try to write codes yourself. Then, in case of any error, you can match your code with the source code provided in the book as well as in the Python Notebooks in the *Resources* folder.

Finally, answer the questions asked in the exercises at the end of each chapter. The solutions to the exercises have been given at the end of the book.

To facilitate the reading process, occasionally, the book presents three types of box-tags in different colors: **Requirements**, **Further Readings**, and **Hands-on Time**. Examples of these boxes are shown below.

Requirements

This box lists all requirements needed to be done before proceeding to the next topic. Generally, it works as a checklist to see if everything is ready before a tutorial.

Further Readings

Here, you will be pointed to some external reference or source that will serve as additional content about the specific **Topic** being studied. In general, it consists of packages, documentations, and cheat sheets.

Hands-on Time

Here, you will be pointed to an external file to train and test all the knowledge acquired about a **Tool** that has been studied. Generally, these files are Jupyter notebooks (.ipynb), Python (.py) files, or documents (.pdf).

The box-tag **Requirements** lists the steps required by the reader after reading one or more topics. **Further Readings** provides relevant references for specific topics to get to know the additional content of the topics. **Hands-on Time** points to practical tools to start working on the specified topics. Follow the instructions given in the box-tags to better understand the topics presented in this book.

About the Author

M. Usman Malik holds a Ph.D. in Computer Science from Normandy University, France, with Artificial Intelligence and Machine Learning being his main areas of research. Muhammad Usman Malik has over five years of industry experience in Data Science and has worked with both private and public sector organizations. He likes to listen to music and play snooker in his free time.

You can follow his Twitter handle: @usman_malikk.

Get in Touch With Us

Feedback from our readers is always welcome.

For general feedback, please send us an email at contact@aipublishing.io and mention the book title in the subject line.

Although we have taken extraordinary care to ensure the accuracy of our content, errors do occur. If you have found an error in this book, we would be grateful if you could report this to us as soon as you can.

If you are interested in becoming an AI Publishing author and if you have expertise in a topic and you are interested in either writing or contributing to a book, please send us an email at author@aipublishing.io.

An Important Note to Our Valued Readers:

Download the Color Images

Our print edition books are available only in black & white at present. However, the digital edition of our books is available in color PDF.

We request you to download the PDF file containing the color images of the screenshots/diagrams used in this book here:

www.aipublishing.io/book-Numpy-python

The typesetting and publishing costs for a color edition are prohibitive. These costs would push the final price of each book to $50, which would make the book less accessible for most beginners.

We are a small company, and we are negotiating with major publishers for a reduction in the publishing price. We are hopeful of a positive outcome sometime soon. In the meantime, we request you to help us with your wholehearted support, feedback, and review.

For the present, we have decided to print all of our books in black & white and provide access to the color version in PDF. This is a decision that would benefit the majority of our readers, as most of them are students. This would also allow beginners to afford our books.

Warning

In Python, indentation is very important. Python indentation is a way of telling a Python interpreter that the group of statements belongs to a particular code block. After each loop or if-condition, be sure to pay close attention to the intent.

Example

```
# Python program showing
# indentation

site = 'aisciences'

if site == 'aisciences':
    print('Logging to www.aisciences.io...')
else:
    print('retype the URL.')
print('All set !')
```

To avoid problems during execution, we advise you to download the codes available on Github by requesting access from the link below. Please have your order number ready for access:

www.aipublishing.io/book-Numpy-python

1

Introduction

In this chapter, you will briefly see what NumPy and Pandas libraries are and their advantages. You will also set up the environment that you will need to run the NumPy and Pandas scripts in this book. The chapter concludes with an optional crash course on the Python programming language.

1.1. What Is NumPy?

NumPy (https://numpy.org/) is one of the most commonly used libraries for numeric and scientific computing. The word NumPy is a portmanteau of two words: Numerical and Python. NumPy is extremely fast and contains support for multiple mathematical domains such as linear algebra, geometry, etc. Therefore, it is extremely important to learn NumPy in case you plan to make a career in data science and data preparation.

The NumPy library stores data in the form of NumPy arrays, which provide extremely fast and memory-efficient data storage. Many advanced data science and machine learning libraries require data to be in the form of NumPy arrays before it can be processed.

A NumPy array has many advantages over regular Python lists. Some of them are listed below:

- NumPy arrays are much faster for insertion, deletion, updating, and reading of data.
- NumPy arrays contain advanced broadcasting functionalities compared with regular Python arrays.
- NumPy arrays come with a lot of methods that support advanced arithmetic and linear algebra options.
- NumPy provides advanced multi-dimensional array slicing capabilities.

In Part I of this book (chapter 2 to chapter 6), you will study various components and use cases of the NumPy library in detail.

You can install the NumPy package in your Python installation via the following pip command.

```
$ pip install numpy
```

If you install the Anaconda distribution (https://bit.ly/3koKSwb) for Python, as you will see in this chapter, the NumPy library will be installed by default.

1.2. Environment Setup and Installation

1.2.1. Windows Setup

The time has come to install Python on Windows using an IDE. We will use Anaconda throughout this book, right from installing Python to writing multithreaded codes. Now let us get going with the installation.

This section explains how you can download and install Anaconda on Windows.

Follow these steps to download and install Anaconda.

1. Open the following URL in your browser.

   https://www.anaconda.com/products/individual

2. The browser will take you to the following webpage. Depending on your OS, select the 64-bit or 32-bit Graphical Installer file for Windows. The file will download within 2–3 minutes based on the speed of your internet.

3. Run the executable file after the download is complete. You will most likely find the downloaded file in your download folder. The installation wizard will open when you run the file, as shown in the following figure. Click the *Next* button.

4. Now click *I Agree* on the **License Agreement** dialog, as shown in the following screenshot.

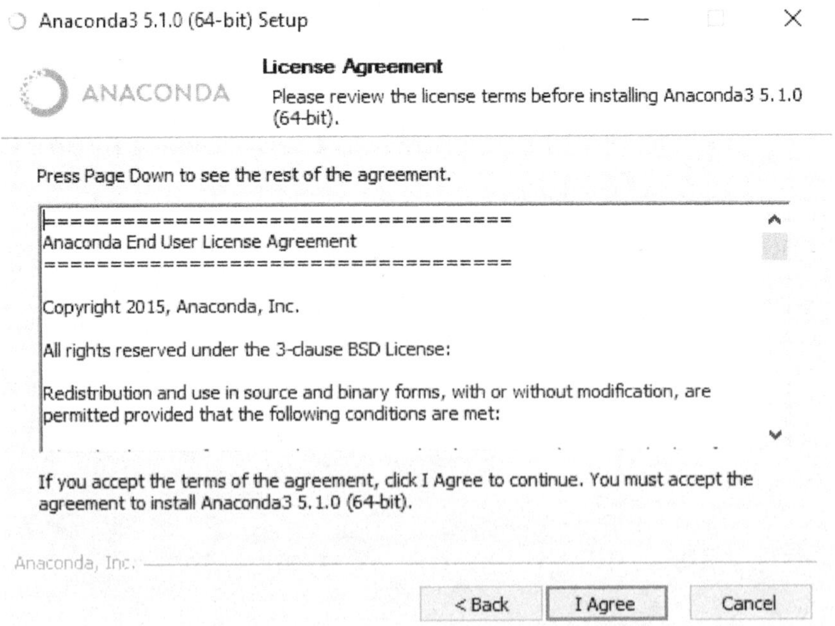

5. Check the *Just Me* radio button from the **Select Installation Type** dialog box. Then, click the *Next* button to continue.

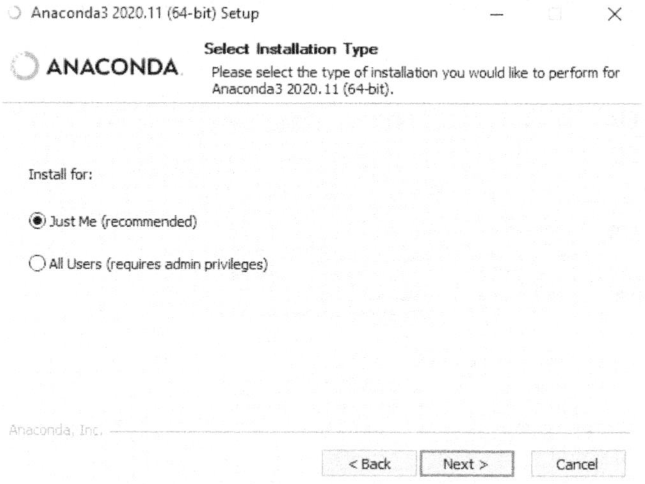

6. Now, the **Choose Install Location** dialog will be displayed. Change the directory if you want, but the default is preferred. The installation folder should have at least 3 GB of free space for Anaconda. Click the *Next* button.

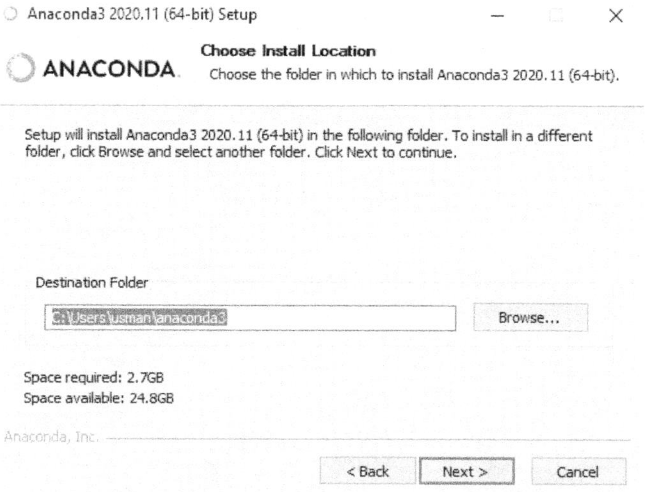

7. Go for the second option, *Register Anaconda as my default Python 3.8,* in the **Advanced Installation Options** dialog box. Click the *Install* button to start the installation, which can take some time to complete.

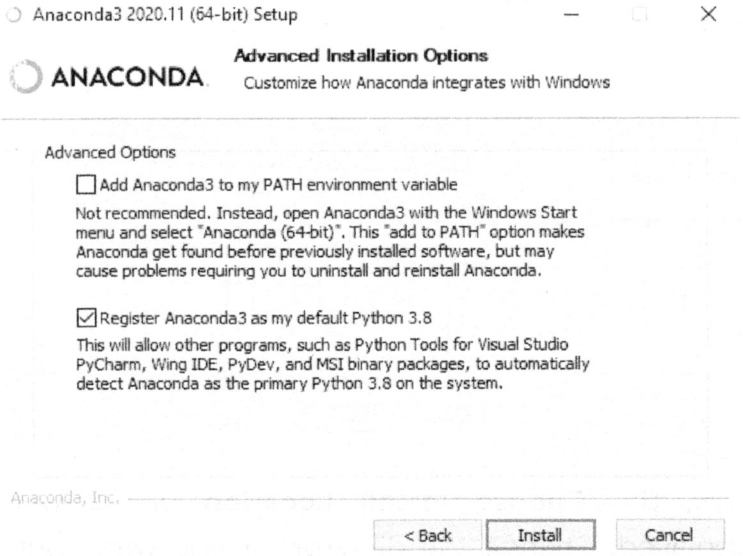

8. Click *Next* once the installation is complete.

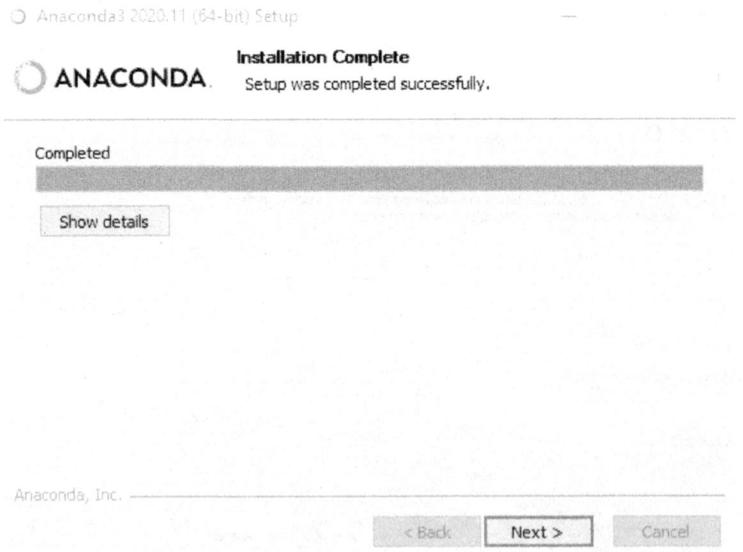

9. Click *Skip* on the ***Microsoft Visual Studio Code Installation*** dialog box.

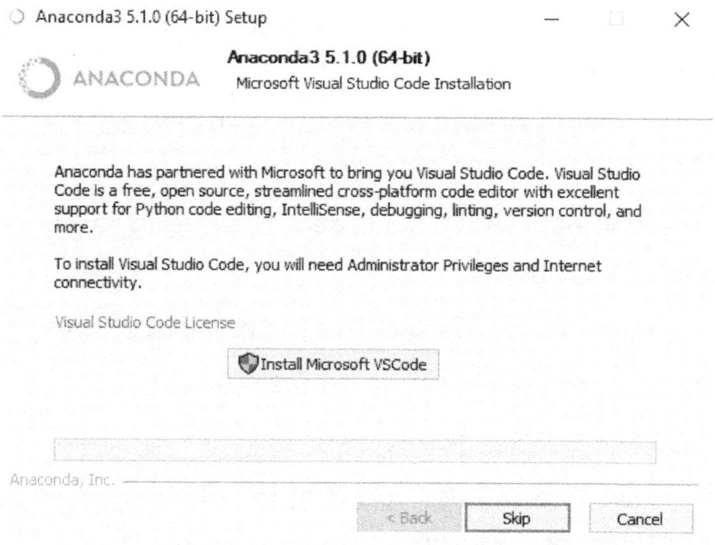

10. You have successfully installed Anaconda on your Windows. Excellent job. The next step is to uncheck both checkboxes on the dialog box. Now, click on the *Finish* button.

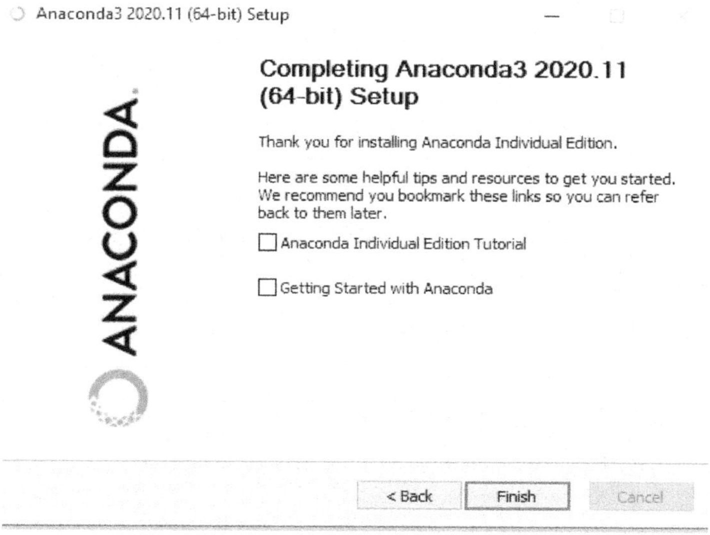

1.2.2. Mac Setup

Anaconda's installation process is almost the same for Mac. It may differ graphically, but you will follow the same steps you followed for Windows. The only difference is that you have to download the executable file, which is compatible with Mac operating system.

This section explains how you can download and install Anaconda on Mac.

Follow these steps to download and install Anaconda.

1. Open the following URL in your browser.

   https://www.anaconda.com/products/individual

2. The browser will take you to the following webpage. Depending on your OS, select the 64-bit or 32-bit Graphical Installer file for macOS. The file will download within 2–3 minutes based on the speed of your internet.

3. Run the executable file after the download is complete. You will most likely find the downloaded file in your download folder. The name of the file should be similar to "Anaconda3-5.1.0-Windows-x86_64." The installation wizard will open when you run the file, as shown in the following figure. Click the *Continue* button.

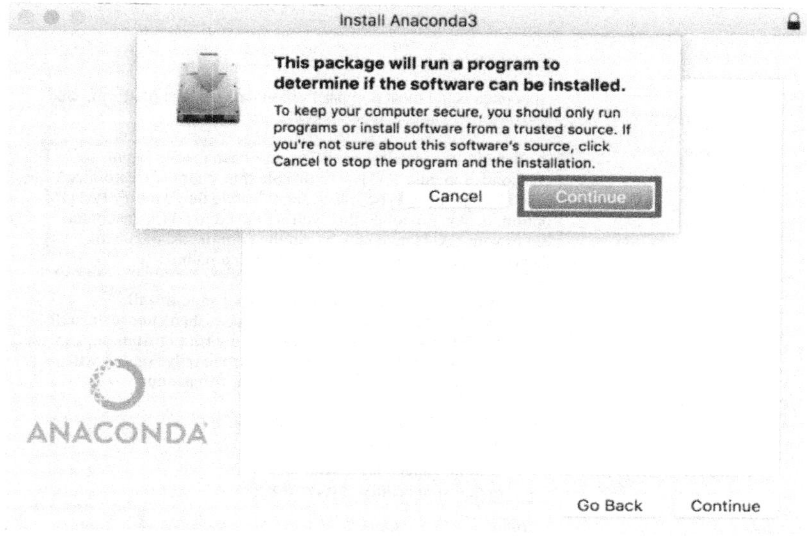

4. Now click *Continue* on the **Welcome to Anaconda 3 Installer** window, as shown in the following screenshot.

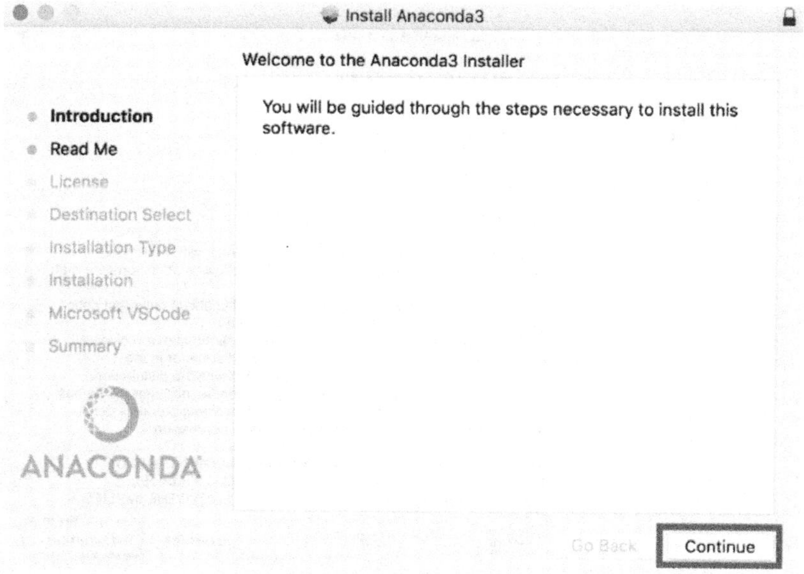

5. The **Important Information** dialog will pop up. Simply click *Continue* to go with the default version, that is, Anaconda 3.

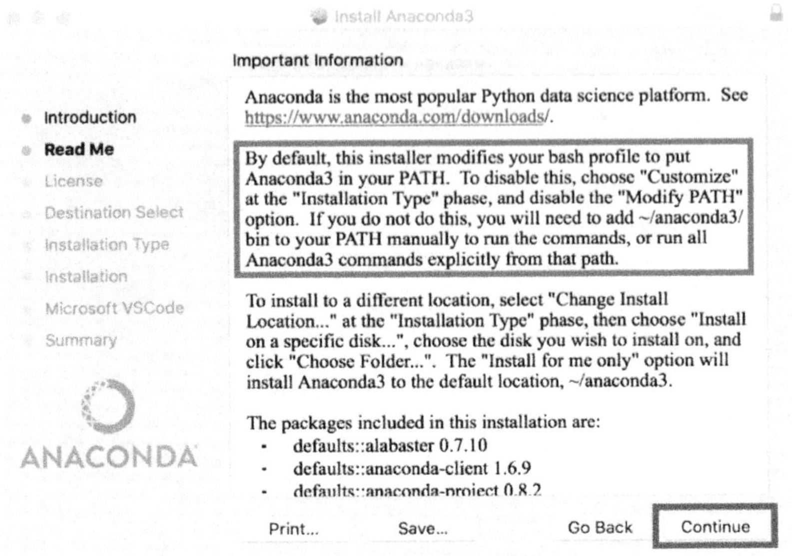

6. Click *Continue* on the **Software License Agreement** dialog.

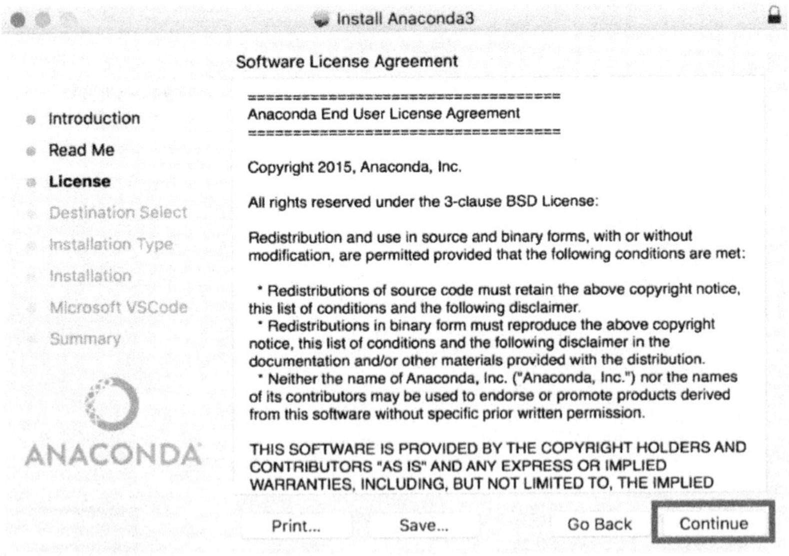

7. It is mandatory to read the license agreement and click the *Agree* button before you can click the *Continue* button again.

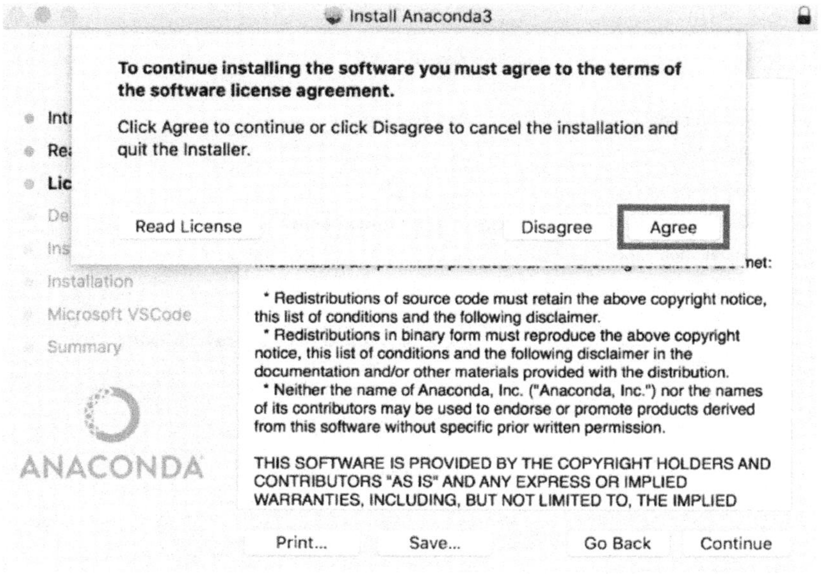

8. Simply click *Install* on the next window that appears.

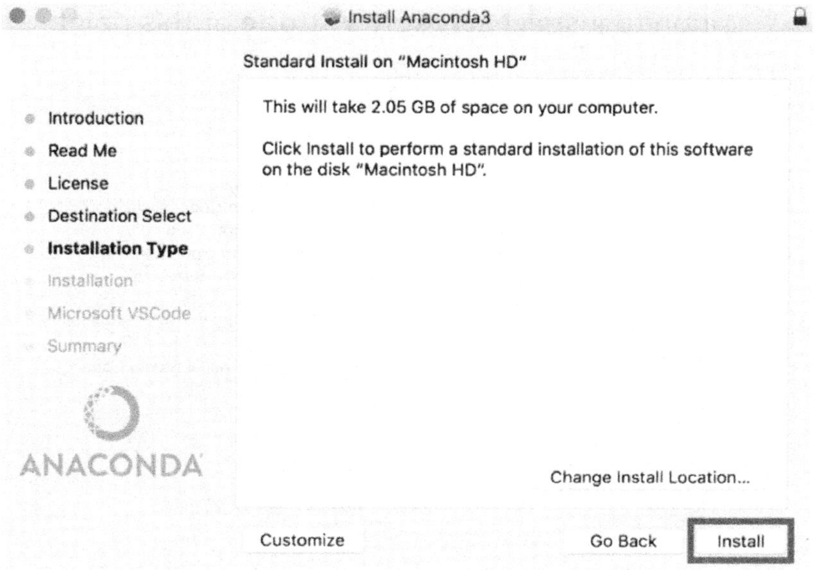

The system will prompt you to give your password. Use the same password you use to log in to your Mac computer. Now, click on *Install Software.*

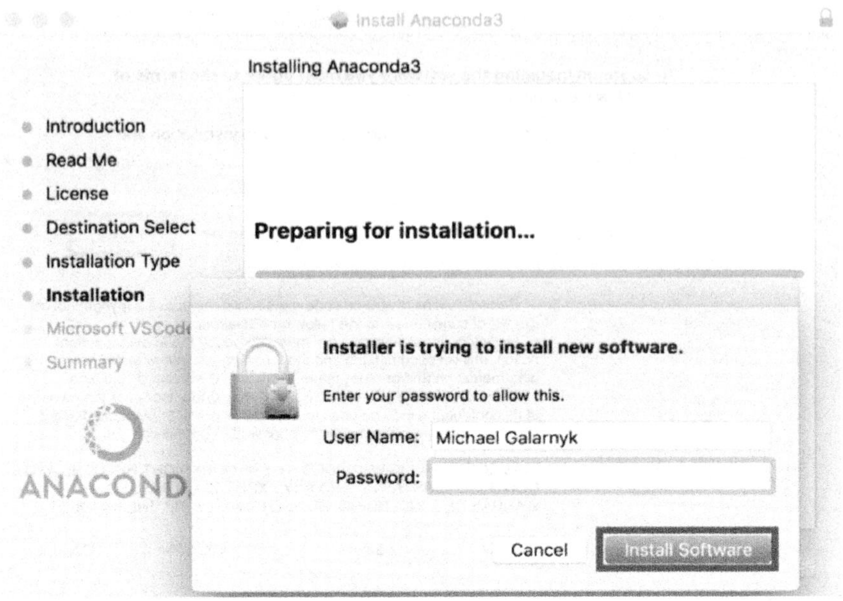

9. Click *Continue* on the next window. You also have the option to install **Microsoft VSCode** at this point.

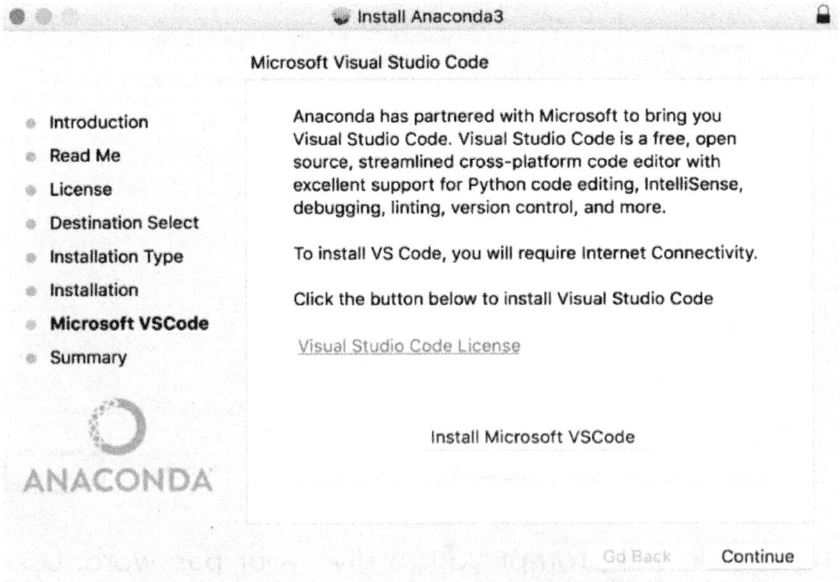

The next screen will display the message that the installation has been completed successfully. Click on the *Close* button to close the installer.

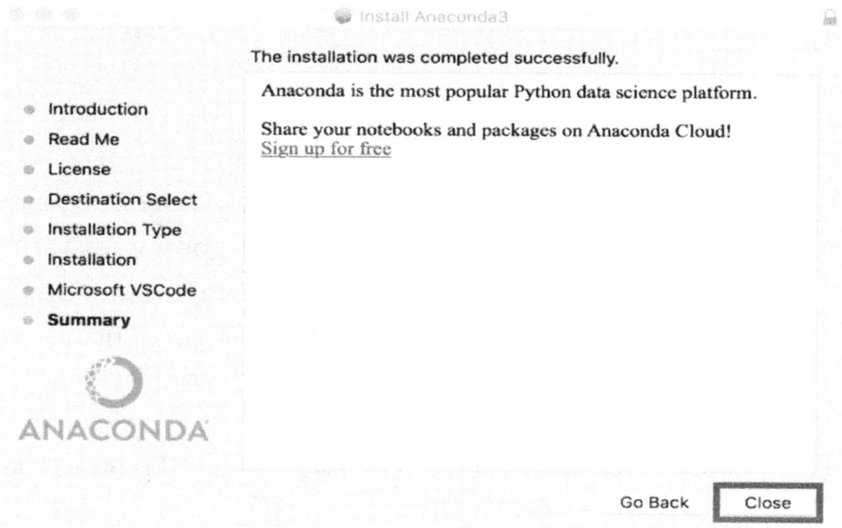

There you have it. You have successfully installed Anaconda on your Mac computer. Now, you can write Python code in Jupyter and Spyder the same way you wrote it in Windows.

1.2.3. Linux Setup

We have used Python's graphical installers for installation on Windows and Mac. However, we will use the command line to install Python on Ubuntu or Linux. Linux is also more resource-friendly, and installation of software is particularly easy as well.

Follow these steps to install Anaconda on Linux (Ubuntu distribution).

1. Go to the following link to copy the installer bash script from the latest available version.

   https://www.anaconda.com/products/individual

2. The second step is to download the installer bash script. Log into your Linux computer and open your terminal. Now, go to /temp directory and download the bash you downloaded from Anaconda's home page using curl.

```
$ cd / tmp

$ curl –o https://repo.anaconda.com.archive/Anaconda3-
5.2.0-Linux-x86_64.sh
```

3. You should also use the cryptographic hash verification through SHA-256 checksum to verify the integrity of the installer.

```
$ sha256sum Anaconda3-5.2.0-Linux-x86_64.sh
```

You will get the following output.

```
09f53738b0cd3bb96f5b1bac488e5528df9906be2480fe61df40e0
    e0d19e3d48 Anaconda3-5.2.0-Linux-x86_64.sh
```

4. The fourth step is to run the Anaconda Script, as shown in the following figure.

```
$ bash Anaconda3-5.2.0-Linux-x86_64.sh
```

The command line will produce the following output. You will be asked to review the license agreement. Keep on pressing *Enter* until you reach the end.

```
Output

Welcome to Anaconda3 5.2.0

In order to continue the installation process, please
    review the license agreement.
Please press Enter to continue
>>>
...
Do you approve the license terms? [yes|No]
```

Type *Yes* when you get to the bottom of the License Agreement.

5. The installer will ask you to choose the installation location after you agree to the license agreement. Simply press *Enter* to choose the default location. You can also specify a different location if you want.

```
Output

Anaconda3 will now be installed on the following
    location: /home/tola/anaconda3

- To confirm the location, press ENTER
- To abort the installation, press CTRL-C
- Otherwise, specify a different location below

[/home/tola/anaconda3] >>>
```

The installation will proceed once you press *Enter.* Once again, you have to be patient as the installation process takes some time to complete.

6. You will receive the following result when the installation is complete. If you wish to use the conda command, type *Yes*.

```
Output
...
Installation finished.
Do you wish the installer to prepend the Anaconda3
    install location to a path in your /home/tola/.
    bashrc? [yes|no]
[no]>>>
```

You will have the option to download the Visual Studio Code at this point, as well. Type *yes* or *no* to install or decline, respectively.

7. Use the following command to activate your brand new installation of Anaconda3.

```
$ source `/.bashrc
```

8. You can also test the installation using the conda command.

```
$ conda list
```

Congratulations. You have successfully installed Anaconda on your Linux system.

1.2.4. Using Google Colab Cloud Environment

In addition to local Python environments such as Anaconda, you can run deep learning applications on Google Colab as well, which is Google's platform for deep learning with GPU support. All the codes in this book have been run using Google Colab. Therefore, I would suggest that you use Google Colab, too.

To run deep learning applications via Google Colab, all you need is a Google/Gmail account. Once you have a Google/Gmail account, you can simply go to:

https://colab.research.google.com/

Next, click on File -> New notebook, as shown in the following screenshot.

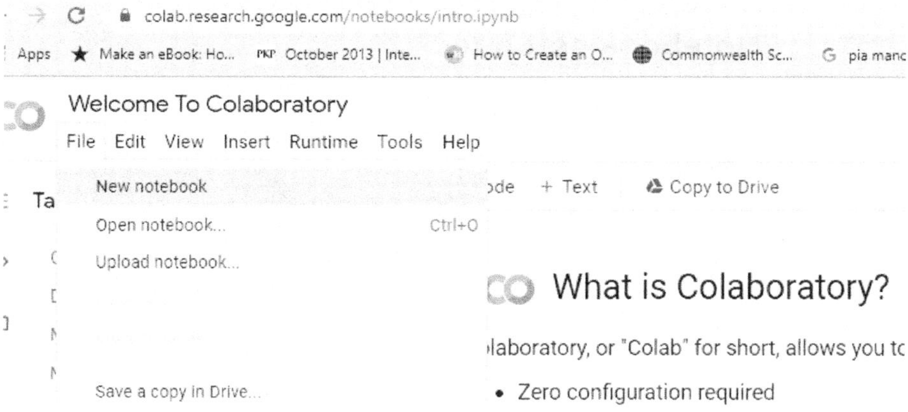

Next, to run your code using GPU, from the top menu, select Runtime -> Change runtime type, as shown in the following screenshot:

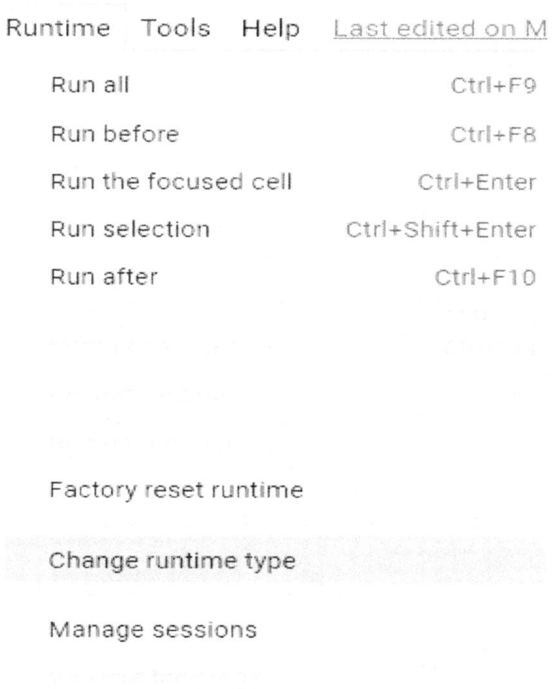

You should see the following window. Here, from the dropdown list, select GPU, and click the *Save* button.

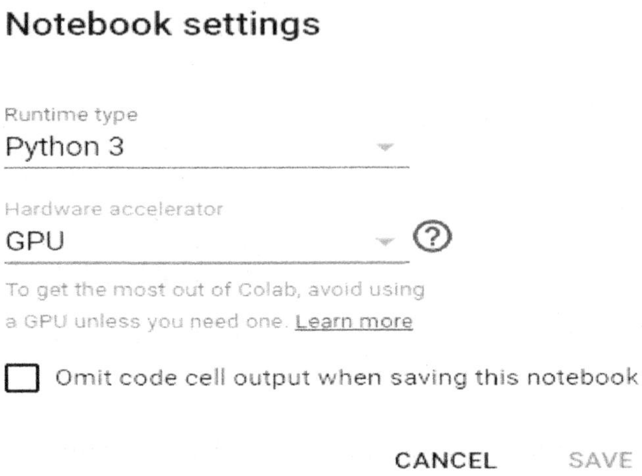

To make sure you are running the latest version of TensorFlow, execute the following script in the Google Colab notebook cell. The following script will update your TensorFlow version.

```
pip install --upgrade tensorflow
```

To check if you are really running TensorFlow version > 2.0, execute the following script.

```
import tensorflow as tf
print(tf.__version__)
```

With Google Cloud, you can import the datasets from your Google Drive. Execute the following script. And click on the link that appears, as shown below:

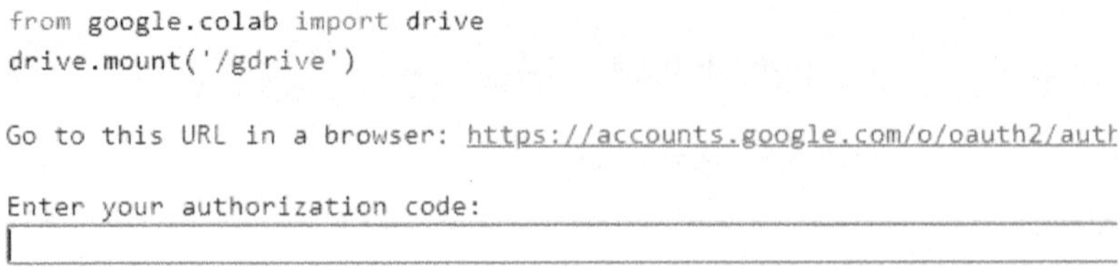

You will be prompted to allow Google Colab to access your Google Drive. Click *Allow* button, as shown below:

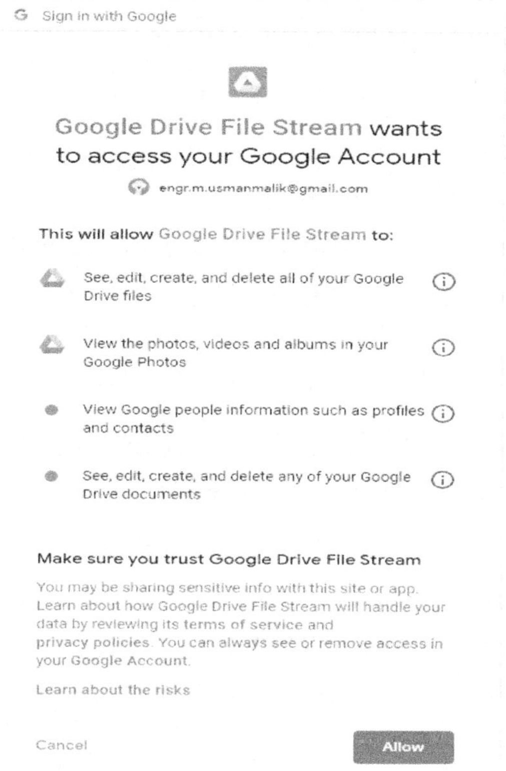

You will see a link appear, as shown in the following image (the link has been blinded here).

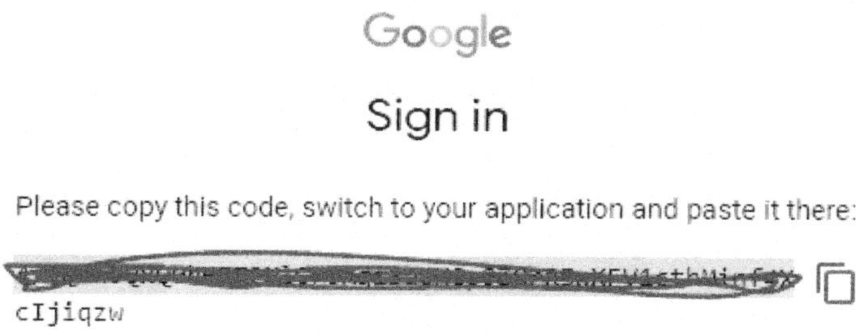

Copy the link and paste it in the empty field in the Google Colab cell, as shown below:

```
from google.colab import drive
drive.mount('/gdrive')

Go to this URL in a browser: https://accounts.google.com/o/oauth2/autt

Enter your authorization code:
```

This way, you can import datasets from your Google Drive to your Google Colab environment.

1.2.5. Writing Your First Program

You have installed Python on your computer now and established a distinctive environment in the form of Anaconda. It's now time to write your first program, i.e., the Hello World!

Start by launching the Anaconda Navigator. First, key in "Anaconda Navigator" in your Windows search box. Next, as shown in the following figure, click on the Anaconda Navigator application icon.

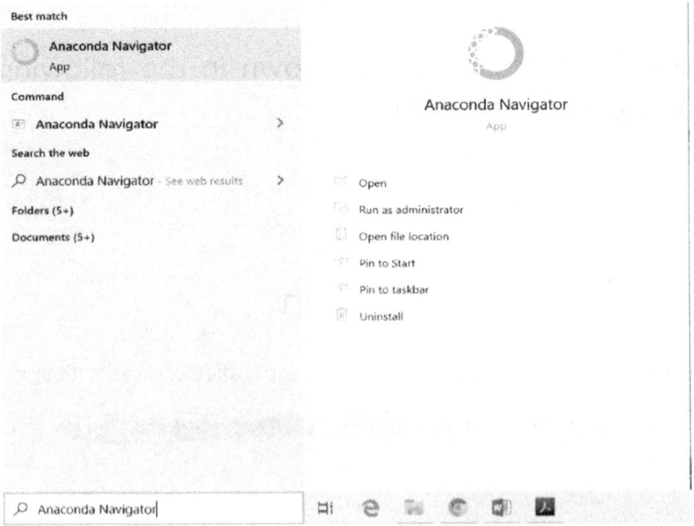

Anaconda's dashboard will open once you click on the application. The dashboard offers you an assortment of tools to write your code. We will use Jupyter Notebook, the most popular of these tools, to write and explain the code throughout this book.

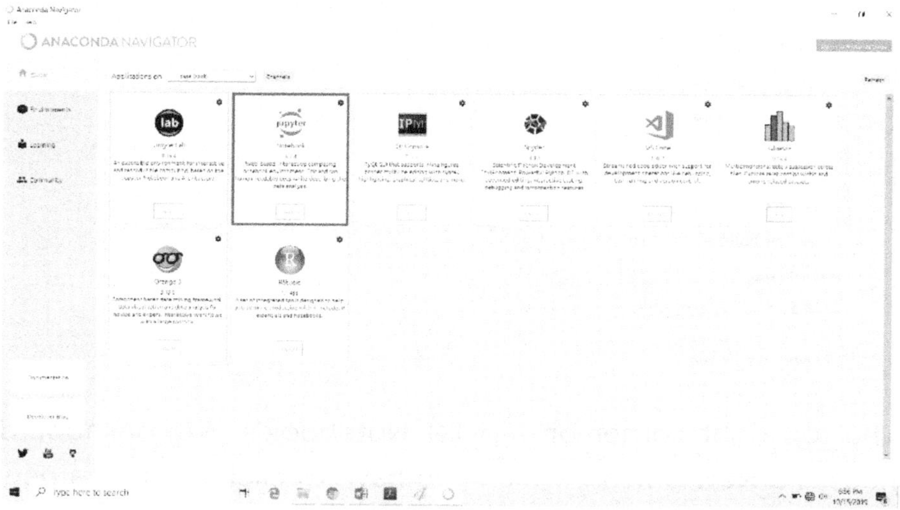

Jupyter Notebook is available in the second position from the top of the dashboard. The key feature of Jupyter Notebook is you can use it even if you don't have internet access, as it runs right in your default browser. Another method to open Jupyter Notebook is to type Jupyter Notebook in the Windows search bar. Subsequently, click on the Jupyter Notebook application. The application will open in a new tab on your browser.

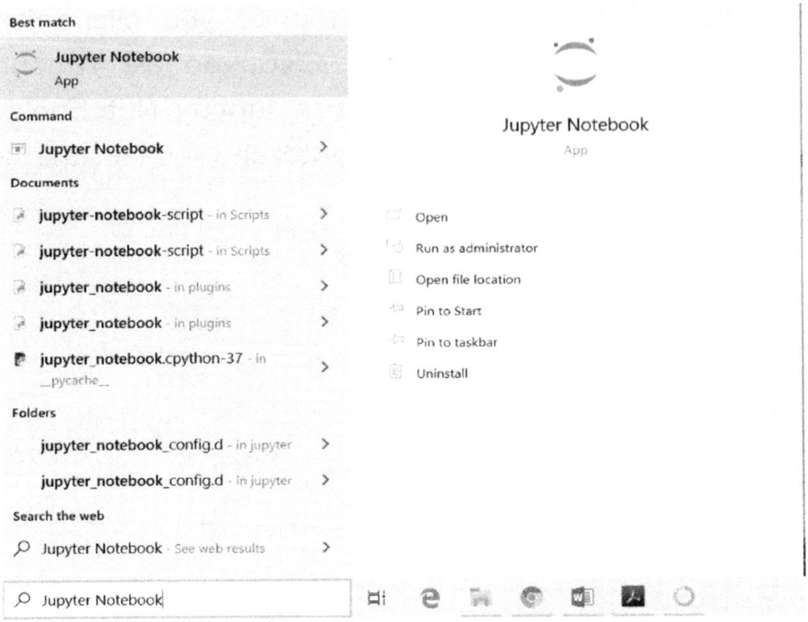

The top right corner of Jupyter Notebook's own dashboard houses a **New** button, which you have to click to open a new document. A dropdown containing several options will appear. Click on *Python 3*.

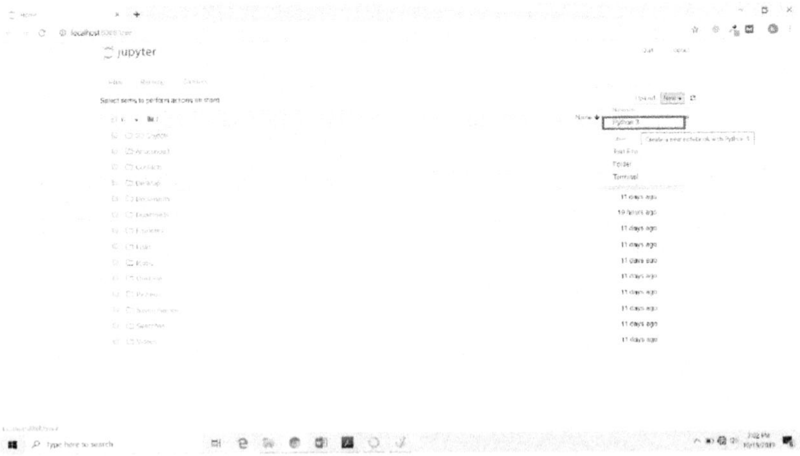

A new Python notebook will appear for you to write your programs. It looks as follows.

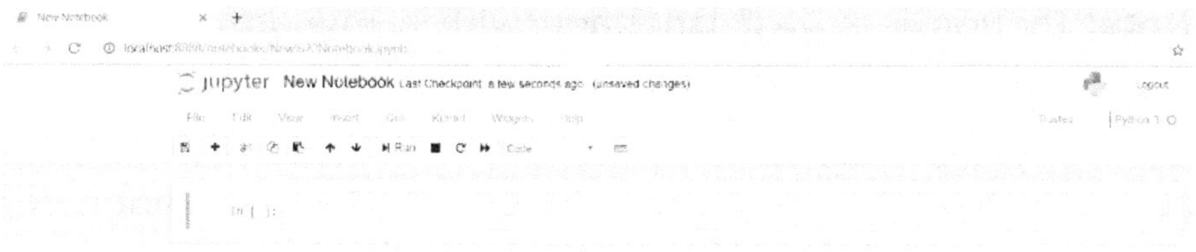

Jupyter Notebook consists of cells, as evident from the above image, making its layout very simple and straightforward. You will write your code inside these cells. Let us write our first ever Python program in Jupyter Notebook.

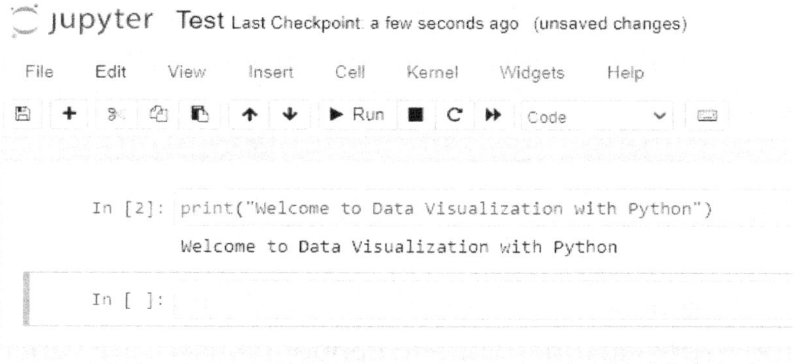

The above script prints a string value in the output using the **print()** method. The **print()** method is used to print any string passed to it on the console. If you see the following output, you have successfully run your first Python program.

Output:

```
Welcome to Data Visualization with Python
```

1.3. Python Crash Course

In this section, you will see a very brief introduction to various Python concepts. You can skip this section if you are already proficient with basic Python concepts. But if you are new to Python, this section can serve as a basic intro to Python.

Note: Python is a vast language with a myriad of features. This section doesn't serve as your complete guide to Python but merely helps get your feet wet with Python. To learn more about Python, you may check its official documentation, for which the link is given at the end of this section.

1.3.1. Python Syntax

Syntax of a language is a set of rules that the developer or the person writing the code must follow for the successful execution of code. Just like natural languages such as English have grammar and spelling rules, programming languages have their own rules.

Let's see some basic Python syntax rules.

Keywords

Every programming language has a specific set of words that perform specific functions and cannot be used as a variable or identifier. Python has the following set of keywords:

False	class	finally	is	return
None	continue	for	lambda	try
True	def	from	nonlocal	while
and	del	global	not	with
as	elif	if	or	yield
assert	else	import	pass	
break	except	in	raise	

For instance, the keyword *class* is used to create a new class in Python (we will see classes in detail in a later chapter).

Furthermore, the *If* keyword creates an if condition. If you try to use any of these keywords as variables, you will see errors.

Python Statements

Statements in Python are the smallest unit of executable code. When you assign a value to an identifier, you basically write a statement. For example, age = 10 is a Python statement. When Python executes this statement, it assigns a value of 10 to the age identifier.

```
age = 10
print(age)
```

The script above has two statements. The first statement assigns a value of 10 to the age identifier. The second statement prints the age identifier.

If your statements are too long, you can span them by enclosing them in parenthesis, braces, or brackets, as shown below:

```
message = ("This is a message "
"it spans multiple lines")

print(message)
```

Output:

```
This is a message it spans multiple lines
```

Another way to write a statement on multiple lines is by adding a backslash (\) at the end of the first line. Look at the following script:

```
message = "This is a message " \
"it spans multiple lines"

print(message)
```

The output is the same as that of the previous script.

Indentation

Indentation is one of those features that distinguish Python from other advanced programming languages such as C++, Java, and C#. In other programming languages, normally, braces ({) are used to define a block of code.

Indentation is used to define a new block of code in Python. A block of code in Python is a set of Python statements that execute together. You will see blocks in action when you study loops and conditional statements.

To define a new block, you have to indent the Python code, one tab (or four spaces) from the left.

```
age = 8
    if age <10:
    print("Age is less than 10")
      print("You do not qualify")
    else:
      print("Age is greater than or equal to 10")
      print("You do qualify")
```

Output:

```
Age is less than 10
You do not qualify
```

In the above code, we define an identifier **age** with a value of 8. We then use the *if* statement and check if the age is less than or not. If age is less than 10, then the first block of code executes, which prints two statements on the console. You can see that code blocks have been indented.

Comments

Comments are used to add notes to a program. Comments do not execute, and you don't have to declare them in the form of statements. Comments are used to explain the code so that if you take a look at the code after a long time, you understand what you did.

Comments can be of two types: Single line comments and double-line comments. To add single line comments, you simply have to add #, as shown below:

```
# The following statement adds two numbers

num = 10 + 20# the result is 30
```

To add multiline comments, you just need to add a # at the start of every line, as shown below:

```
#This is comment 1
#This is comment 2
#This is comment 3
```

1.3.2. Python Variables and Data Types

Data types in a programming language refer to the type of data that the language is capable of processing. The following are the major data types supported by Python:

a. Strings
b. Integers
c. Floating Point Numbers
d. Booleans
e. Lists
f. Tuples
g. Dictionaries

A variable is an alias for the memory address where actual data is stored. The data or the values stored at a memory address can be accessed and updated via the variable name. Unlike other programming languages like C++, Java, and C#, Python is loosely typed, which means that you don't have to define the data type while creating a variable. Instead, the type of data is evaluated at runtime.

The example below demonstrates how to create different data types and how to store them in their corresponding variables. The script also prints the type of the variables via the **type()** function.

Script 1:

```
# A string Variable
    first_name = "Joseph"
    print(type(first_name))

# An Integer Variable
    age = 20
    print(type(age))

# A floating point variable
    weight = 70.35
    print(type(weight))

# A Boolean variable
    married = False
    print(type(married))

#List
    cars = ["Honda", "Toyota", "Suzuki"]
    print(type(cars))

#Tuples
    days = ("Sunday", "Monday", "Tuesday", "Wednesday",
    "Thursday", "Friday", "Saturday")
    print(type(days))

#Dictionaries
    days2 = {1:"Sunday", 2:"Monday", 3:"Tuesday",
    4:"Wednesday", 5:"Thursday", 6:"Friday", 7:"Saturday"}
    print(type(days2))
```

Output:

```
<class 'str'>
<class 'int'>
<class 'float'>
<class 'bool'>
<class 'list'>
<class 'tuple'>
<class 'dict'>
```

1.3.3. Python Operators

Python programming language contains the following types of operators:

a. Arithmetic Operators
b. Logical Operators
c. Comparison Operators
d. Assignment Operators
e. Membership Operators

Let's briefly review each of these types of operators.

Arithmetic Operators

Arithmetic operators are used to execute arithmetic operations in Python. The following table summarizes the arithmetic operators supported by Python. Suppose X = 20 and Y = 10.

Operator Name	Symbol	Functionality	Example
Addition	+	Adds the operands on either side	X+ Y= 30
Subtraction	–	Subtracts the operands on either side	X –Y= 10

Multiplication	*	Multiplies the operands on either side	X * Y= 200
Division	/	Divides the operand on the left by the one on the right	X / Y= 2.0
Modulus	%	Divides the operand on the left by the one on the right and returns the remainder	X % Y= 0
Exponent	**	Takes exponent of the operand on the left to the power of right	X ** Y = 1024 x e^{10}

Here is an example of arithmetic operators with output:

Script 2:

```
X = 20
Y = 10
print(X + Y)
print(X - Y)
print(X * Y)
print(X / Y)
print(X ** Y)
```

Output:

```
30
10
200
2.0
10240000000000
```

Logical Operators

Logical operators are used to perform logical `AND`, `OR`, and `NOT` operations in Python. The following table summarizes the logical operators. Here, `X` is `True`, and `Y` is `False`.

Operator	Symbol	Functionality	Example
Logical AND	and	If both the operands are true, then the condition becomes true.	(X and Y) = False
Logical OR	or	If any of the two operands are true, then the condition becomes true.	(X or Y) = True
Logical NOT	not	Used to reverse the logical state of its operand.	not(X and Y) = True

Here is an example that explains the usage of the Python logical operators.

Script 3:

```
X = True
Y = False
print(X and Y)
print(X or Y)
print(not(X and Y))


Output:
False
True
True
```

Comparison Operators

Comparison operators, as the name suggests, are used to compare two or more than two operands. Depending upon the relation between the operands, comparison operators return Boolean values. The following table summarizes comparison operators in Python. Here, X is 20, and Y is 35.

Operator	Symbol	Description	Example
Equality	==	Returns true if values of both the operands are equal	(X == Y) = false
Inequality	!=	Returns true if values of both the operands are not equal	(X = Y) = true
Greater than	>	Returns true if the value of the left operand is greater than the right one	(X> Y) = False
Smaller than	<	Returns true if the value of the left operand is smaller than the right one	(X< Y) = True
Greater than or equal to	>=	Returns true if the value of the left operand is greater than or equal to the right one	(X > =Y) = False
Smaller than or equal to	<=	Returns true if the value of the left operand is smaller than or equal to the right one	(X<= Y) = True

The comparison operators have been demonstrated in action in the following example:

Script 4

```
X = 20
Y = 35

print(X == Y)
print(X != Y)
print(X > Y)
print(X < Y)
print(X >= Y)
print(X <= Y)
```

Output:

```
False
True
False
True
False
True
```

Assignment Operators

Assignment operators are used to assign values to variables. The following table summarizes the assignment operators. Here, X is 20, and Y is equal to 10.

Operator	Symbol	Description	Example
Assignment	=	Used to assign the value of the right operand to the left operand	R = X+ Y assigns 30 to R
Add and assign	+=	Adds the operands on either side and assigns the result to the left operand	X += Y assigns 30 to X
Subtract and assign	-=	Subtracts the operand on the right from the operand on the left and assigns the result to the left operand	X -= Y assigns 10 to X
Multiply and Assign	*=	Multiplies the operands on either side and assigns the result to the left operand	X *= Y assigns 200 to X
Divide and Assign	/=	Divides the operands on the left by the right and assigns the result to the left operand	X/= Y assigns 2 to X

Take modulus and assign	%=	Divides the operands on the left by the right and assigns the remainder to the left operand	X %= Y assigns 0 to X
Take exponent and assign	**=	Takes exponent of the operand on the left to the power of right and assigns the remainder to the left operand	X **= Y assigns 1024 x e^{10} to X

Take a look at the script below to see Python assignment operators in action.

Script 5:

```
X = 20; Y = 10
R = X + Y
print(R)

X = 20;
Y = 10
X += Y
print(X)

X = 20;
Y = 10
X -= Y
print(X)

X = 20;
Y = 10
X *= Y
print(X)

X = 20;
Y = 10
X /= Y
print(X)
```

```
X = 20;
Y = 10
X %= Y
print(X)

X = 20;
Y = 10
X **= Y
print(X)
```

Output:

```
30
30
10
200
2.0
0
10240000000000
```

Membership Operators

Membership operators are used to find if an item is a member of a collection of items or not. There are two types of membership operators: the **in** operator and the **not in** operator. The following script shows **an** operator in action.

Script 6:

```
days = ("Sunday", "Monday", "Tuesday", "Wednesday",
    "Thursday", "Friday", "Saturday")
print('Sunday' in days)
```

Output:

```
True
```

And here is an example of the **not in** operator.

Script 7:

```
days = ("Sunday", "Monday", "Tuesday", "Wednesday",
   "Thursday", "Friday", "Saturday")
print('Xunday' not in days)
```

Output:

```
True
```

1.3.4. Conditional Statements

Conditional statements in Python are used to implement conditional logic in Python. Conditional statements help you decide whether to execute a certain code block or not. There are three main types of conditional statements in Python:

a. If statement

b. If-else statement

c. If-elif statement

IF Statement

If you have to check for a single condition and you do not concern yourself about the alternate condition, you can use the **if** statement. For instance, if you want to check if 10 is greater than 5 and based on that you want to print a statement, you can use the if statement. The condition evaluated by the **if** statement returns a Boolean value. If the condition evaluated by the **if** statement is true, the code block that follows the **if** statement executes. It is important to mention that in Python, a new code block starts at a new line with a tab indented from the left when compared with the outer block.

In the following example, the condition 10 > 5 is evaluated, which returns true. Hence, the code block that follows the **if** statement executes, and a message is printed on the console.

Script 8:

```
# The if statement

   if 10 > 5:
     print("Ten is greater than 10")
```

Output:

```
Ten is greater than 10
```

IF-Else Statement

The **If-else** statement comes in handy when you want to execute an alternate piece of code in case the condition for the *if* statement returns false. For instance, in the following example, the condition 5 < 10 will return false. Hence, the code block that follows the **else** statement will execute.

Script 9:

```
# if-else statement

   if 5 > 10:
     print("5 is greater than 10")
   else:
     print("10 is greater than 5")
```

Output:

```
10 is greater than 5
```

IF-Elif Statement

The **if-elif** statement comes handy when you have to evaluate multiple conditions. For instance, in the following example, we first check if 5 > 10, which evaluates to false. Next, an **elif** statement evaluates the condition 8 < 4, which also returns false. Hence, the code block that follows the last **else** statement executes.

Script 10:

```
#if-elif and else

    if 5 > 10:
      print("5 is greater than 10")
    elif 8 < 4:
      print("8 is smaller than 4")
    else:
      print("5 is not greater than 10 and 8 is not smaller
    than 4")
```

Output:

```
5 is not greater than 10 and 8 is not smaller than 4
```

1.3.5. Iteration Statements

Iteration statements, also known as loops, are used to iteratively execute a certain piece of code. There are two main types of iteration statements in Python.

a. For loop

b. While Loop

For Loop

The **for loop** is used to iteratively execute a piece of code a certain number of times. You should use **for loop** when you exactly know the number of iterations or repetitions for which you want to run your code. A **for loop** iterates over a collection of items. In the following example, we create a collection of five integers using the **range()** method. Next, a **for loop** iterates five times and prints each integer in the collection.

Script 11:

```
items = range(5)
    for item in items:
      print(item)
```

Output:

```
0
1
2
3
4
```

While Loop

The **while loop** keeps executing a certain piece of code unless the evaluation condition becomes false. For instance, the **while loop** in the following script keeps executing unless variable c becomes greater than 10.

Script 12:

```
c = 0
    while c < 10:
      print(c)
      c = c +1
```

Output:

```
0
1
2
3
4
5
6
7
8
9
```

1.3.6. Functions

Functions, in any programming language, are used to implement a piece of code that is required to be executed multiple times at different locations in the code. In such cases, instead of writing long pieces of code, again and again, you can simply define a function that contains the piece of code, and then you can call the function wherever you want in the code.

To create a function in Python, the *def* keyword is used, followed by the name of the function and opening and closing parenthesis.

Once a function is defined, you have to call it to execute the code inside a function body. To call a function, you simply have to specify the name of the function followed by opening and closing parenthesis. In the following script, we create a function named **myfunc** which prints a simple statement on the console using the **print()** method.

Script 13:

```
def myfunc():
     print("This is a simple function")

  ### function call
  myfunc()
```

Output:

```
This is a simple function
```

You can also pass values to a function. The values are passed inside the parenthesis of the function call. However, you must specify the parameter name in the function definition, too. In the following script, we define a function named

myfuncparam(). The function accepts one parameter, i.e., **num**. The value passed in the parenthesis of the function call will be stored in this **num** variable and will be printed by the **print()** method inside the **myfuncparam()** method.

Script 14:

```
def myfuncparam(num):
     print("This is a function with parameter value: "+num)

### function call
   myfuncparam("Parameter 1")
```

Output:

```
This is a function with parameter value: Parameter 1
```

Finally, a function can also return values to the function call. To do so, you simply have to use the return keyword followed by the value that you want to return. In the following script, the **myreturnfunc()** function returns a string value to the calling function.

Script 15:

```
def myreturnfunc():
     return "This function returns a value"

   val = myreturnfunc()
   print(val)
```

Output:

```
This function returns a value
```

1.3.7. Objects and Classes

Python supports object-oriented programming (OOP). In OOP, any entity that can perform some function and have some attributes is implemented in the form of an object.

For instance, a car can be implemented as an object since a car has some attributes such as price, color, model and can perform some functions such as drive car, change gear, stop car, etc.

Similarly, a fruit can also be implemented as an object since a fruit has a price, name and you can eat a fruit, grow a fruit, and perform functions with a fruit.

To create an object, you first have to define a class. For instance, in the following example, a class **Fruit** has been defined. The class has two attributes **name** and **price** and one method, **eat_fruit()**. Next, we create an object **f** of class Fruit and then call the **eat_fruit()** method from the **f** object. We also access the **name** and **price** attributes of the **f** object and print them on the console.

Script 16:

```
class Fruit:

     name = "apple"
     price = 10

     def eat_fruit(self):
       print("Fruit has been eaten")


   f = Fruit()
   f.eat_fruit()
   print(f.name)
   print(f.price)
```

Output:

```
Fruit has been eaten
apple
10
```

A class in Python can have a special method called a *constructor*. The name of the constructor method in Python is **`__init__()`**. The constructor is called whenever an object of a class is created. Look at the following example to see the constructor in action.

Script 17:

```
class Fruit:

     name = "apple"
     price = 10

     def __init__(self, fruit_name, fruit_price):
       Fruit.name = fruit_name
       Fruit.price = fruit_price

     def eat_fruit(self):
       print("Fruit has been eaten")


   f = Fruit("Orange", 15)
   f.eat_fruit()
   print(f.name)
   print(f.price)
```

Output:

```
Fruit has been eaten
Orange
15
```

Further Readings - Python [1]

To study more about Python, please check Python 3 Official Documentation (https://bit.ly/3rfaLke). Get used to searching and reading this documentation. It is a great resource of knowledge.

Hands-on Time - Exercise

Now, it is your turn. Follow the instructions in **the exercises below** to check your understanding of the basic Python concepts. The answers to these questions are given at the end of the book.

Exercise 1.1

Question 1

Which iteration should be used when you want to repeatedly execute a code specific number of times?

A. For Loop

B. While Loop

C. Both A & B

D. None of the above

Question 2

What is the maximum number of values that a function can return in Python?

A. Single Value

B. Double Value

C. More than two values

D. None

Question 3

Which of the following membership operators are supported by Python?

A. In

B. Out

C. Not In

D. Both A and C

Exercise 1.2

Print the table of integer 9 using a while loop.

2

NumPy Basics

2.1. Introduction to NumPy Arrays

The main data structure in the NumPy library is the NumPy array, which is an extremely fast and memory-efficient data structure. The NumPy array is much faster than the common Python list and provides vectorized matrix operations.

In this chapter, you will see the different data types that you can store in a NumPy array, the different ways to create the NumPy arrays, how you can access items in a NumPy array, and how to add or remove items from a NumPy array.

2.2. NumPy Data Types

The NumPy library supports all the default Python data types in addition to some of its intrinsic data types. This means that the default Python data types, e.g., strings, integers, floats, Booleans, and complex data types, can be stored in NumPy arrays.

You can check the data type in a NumPy array using the dtypeprperty. You will see the different ways of creating NumPy arrays in detail in the next section.

Here, we will show you the array() function and then print the type of the NumPy array using the dtype property. Here is an example:

Script 1:

```
importnumpyasnp

my_array = np.array([10,12,14,16,20,25])

print(my_array)
print(my_array.dtype)
print(my_array.dtype.itemsize)
```

The script above defines a NumPy array with six integers. Next, the array type is displayed via the dtype attribute. Finally, the size of each item in the array (in bytes) is displayed via the itemsize attribute.

The output below prints the array and the type of the items in the array, i.e., int32 (integer type), followed by the size of each item in the array, which is 4 bytes (32 bits).

Output:

```
[10 12 14 16 20 25]
int32
4
```

The Python NumPy library supports the following data types including the default Python types.

- i - integer
- b - boolean
- u - unsigned integer
- f - float
- c - complex float

- m - timedelta
- M - datetime
- o - object
- S - string
- U - Unicode string
- V - fixed chunk of memory for other type (void)

Let's see another example of how Python stores text. The following script creates a NumPy array with three text items and displays the data type and size of each item.

Script 2:

```
importnumpyasnp

my_array = np.array(["Red", "Green", "Orange"])

print(my_array)
print(my_array.dtype)
print(my_array.dtype.itemsize)
```

The output below shows that NumPy stores text in the form of Unicode string data type denoted by U. Here, the digit 6 represents the item with the most number of characters.

Output:

```
['Red' 'Green' 'Orange']
<U6
24
```

Though the NumPy array is intelligent enough to guess the data type of items stored in it, this is not always the case. For instance, in the following script, you store some dates in a NumPy array. Since the dates are stored in the form of texts (enclosed in double quotations), by default, the NumPy array treats the dates as text. Hence, if you print the data type of the items stored, you will see that it will be a Unicode string (U10).

Script 3:

```
importnumpyasnp

my_array = np.array(["1990-10-04", "1989-05-06", "1990-11-
    04"])

print(my_array)
print(my_array.dtype)
print(my_array.dtype.itemsize)
```

Output:

```
['1990-10-04' '1989-05-06' '1990-11-04']
<U10
40
```

You can convert data types in the NumPy array to other data types via the astype() method. But first, you need to specify the target data type in the astype() method.

For instance, the following script converts the array you created in the previous script to the datetime data type. You can see that "M" is passed as a parameter value to the astype() function. "M" stands for the datetime data type as aforementioned.

Script 4:

```
my_array3 = my_array.astype("M")

print(my_array3.dtype)
print(my_array3.dtype.itemsize)
```

Output:

```
datetime64[D]
8
```

In addition to converting arrays from one type to another, you can also specify the data type for a NumPy array at the time of definition via the dtype parameter.

For instance, in the following script, you specify "M" as the value for the dtype parameter, which tells the Python interpreter that the items must be stored as datatime values.

Script 5:

```
importnumpyasnp

my_array = np.array(["1990-10-04", "1989-05-06", "1990-11-
    04"], dtype = "M")

print(my_array)
print(my_array.dtype)
print(my_array.dtype.itemsize)
```

Output:

```
['1990-10-04' '1989-05-06' '1990-11-04']
datetime64[D]
8
```

2.3. Creating NumPy Arrays

Depending on the type of data you need inside your NumPy array, different methods can be used to create a NumPy array.

2.3.1. Using Array Method

To create a NumPy array, you can pass a list to the **`array()`** method of the NumPy module, as shown below:

Script 6:

```
importnumpyasnp
nums_list = [10,12,14,16,20]
nums_array = np.array(nums_list)
type(nums_array)
```

Output:

```
numpy.ndarray
```

You can also create a multi-dimensional NumPy array. To do so, you need to create a list of lists where each internal list corresponds to the row in a two-dimensional array. Here is an example of how to create a two-dimensional array using the **array()** method.

Script 7:

```
row1 = [10,12,13]
row2 = [45,32,16]
row3 = [45,32,16]

nums_2d = np.array([row1, row2, row3])
nums_2d.shape
```

Output:

```
(3, 3)
```

2.3.2. Using Arrange Method

With the **arrange ()** method, you can create a NumPy array that contains a range of integers. The first parameter to the arrange method is the lower bound, and the second parameter is the upper bound. The lower bound is included in the array. However, the upper bound is not included. The following script creates a NumPy array with integers 5 to 10.

Script 8:

```
nums_arr = np.arange(5,11)
print(nums_arr)
```

Output:

```
[ 5 6 7 8 9 10]
```

You can also specify the step as a third parameter in the **arrange()** function. A step defines the distance between two consecutive points in the array. The following script creates a NumPy array from 5 to 11 with a step size of 2.

Script 9:

```
nums_arr = np.arange(5,12,2)
print(nums_arr)
```

Output:

```
[ 5 7 9 11]
```

2.3.3. Using Ones Method

The **ones()** method can be used to create a NumPy array of all ones. Here is an example.

Script 10:

```
ones_array = np.ones(6)
print(ones_array)
```

Output:

```
[1. 1. 1. 1. 1. 1.]
```

You can create a two-dimensional array of all ones by passing the number of rows and columns as the first and second parameters of the **ones()** method, as shown below:

Script 11:

```
ones_array = np.ones((6,4))
print(ones_array)
```

Output:

```
[[1. 1. 1. 1.]
 [1. 1. 1. 1.]
 [1. 1. 1. 1.]
 [1. 1. 1. 1.]
 [1. 1. 1. 1.]
 [1. 1. 1. 1.]]
```

2.3.4. Using Zeros Method

The **zeros()** method can be used to create a NumPy array of all zeros. Here is an example.

Script 12:

```
zeros_array = np.zeros(6)
print(zeros_array)
```

Output:

```
[0. 0. 0. 0. 0. 0.]
```

You can create a two-dimensional array of all zeros by passing the number of rows and columns as the first and second parameters of the **zeros()** method, as shown below:

Script 13:

```
zeros_array = np.zeros((6,4))
print(zeros_array)
```

Output:

```
[[0. 0. 0. 0.]
 [0. 0. 0. 0.]
 [0. 0. 0. 0.]
 [0. 0. 0. 0.]
 [0. 0. 0. 0.]
 [0. 0. 0. 0.]]
```

2.3.5. Using Eyes Method

The **eye()** method is used to create an identity matrix in the form of a two-dimensional NumPy array. An identity matrix contains 1s along the diagonal, while the rest of the elements are 0 in the array.

Script 14:

```
eyes_array = np.eye(5)
print(eyes_array)
```

Output:

```
[[1. 0. 0. 0. 0.]
 [0. 1. 0. 0. 0.]
 [0. 0. 1. 0. 0.]
 [0. 0. 0. 1. 0.]
 [0. 0. 0. 0. 1.]]
```

2.3.6. Using Random Method

The **random.rand()** function from the NumPy module can be used to create a NumPy array with uniform distribution.

Script 15:

```
uniform_random = np.random.rand(4, 5)
print(uniform_random)
```

Output:

```
[[0.36728531 0.25376281 0.05039624 0.96432236 0.08579293]
 [0.29194804 0.93016399 0.88781312 0.50209692 0.63069239]
 [0.99952044 0.44384871 0.46041845 0.10246553 0.53461098]
 [0.75817916 0.36505441 0.01683344 0.9887365 0.21490949]]
```

The **random.randn()** function from the NumPy module can be used to create a NumPy array with normal distribution, as shown in the following example.

Script 16:

```
normal_random = np.random.randn(4, 5)
print(uniform_random)
```

Output:

```
[[0.36728531 0.25376281 0.05039624 0.96432236 0.08579293]
 [0.29194804 0.93016399 0.88781312 0.50209692 0.63069239]
 [0.99952044 0.44384871 0.46041845 0.10246553 0.53461098]
 [0.75817916 0.36505441 0.01683344 0.9887365 0.21490949]]
```

Finally, the **random.randint()** function from the NumPy module can be used to create a NumPy array with random integers between a certain range. The first parameter to the **randint()** function specifies the lower bound, the second parameter specifies the upper bound, and the last parameter specifies the number of random integers to generate between the range. The following example generates five random integers between 5 and 50.

Script 17:

```
integer_random = np.random.randint(10, 50, 5)
print(integer_random)
```

Output:

```
[25 49 21 35 17]
```

2.4. Printing NumPy Arrays

Depending on the dimensions, there are various ways to display the NumPy arrays.

The simplest way to print a NumPy array is to pass the array to the print method, as you have already seen in the previous section. An example is given below:

Script 18:

```
importnumpyasnp

my_array = np.array([10,12,14,16,20,25])
print(my_array)
```

Output:

```
[10 12 14 16 20 25]
```

You can also use loops to display items in a NumPy array. It is a good idea to know the dimensions of a NumPy array before printing the array on the console. To see the dimensions of a NumPy array, you can use the ndim attribute, which prints the number of dimensions for a NumPy array. To see the shape of your NumPy array, you can use the shape attribute.

Script 19:

```
print(my_array.ndim)
print(my_array.shape)
```

The script shows that our array is one-dimensional. The shape is (6,), which means our array is a vector with 6 items.

Output:

```
1
(6,)
```

To print items in a one-dimensional NumPy array, you can use a single foreach loop, as shown below:

Script 20:

```
foriinmy_array:
print(i)
```

Output:

```
10
12
14
16
20
25
```

Now, let's see another example of how you can use the foreach loop to print items in a two-dimensional NumPy array.

The following script creates a two-dimensional NumPy array with four rows and five columns. The array contains random integers between 1 and 10. The array is then printed on the console.

Script 21:

```
integer_random = np.random.randint(1,11, size=(4, 5))
print(integer_random)
```

In the output below, you can see your newly created array.

Output:

```
[[ 7 7 10 9 8]
 [ 6 10 2 5 9]
 [ 2 9 2 10 2]
 [ 9 6 3 2 1]]
```

Let's now try to see the number of dimensions and shape of our NumPy array.

Script 22:

```
print(integer_random.ndim)
print(integer_random.shape)
```

The output below shows that our array has two dimensions and the shape of the array is (4,5), which refers to four rows and five columns.

Output:

```
2
(4, 5)
```

To traverse through items in a two-dimensional NumPy array, you need two foreach loops: one for each row and the other for each column in the row.

Let's first use one for loop to print items in our two-dimensional NumPy array.

Script 23:

```
foriinmy_array:
print(i)
```

The output shows all the rows from our two-dimensional NumPy array.

Output:

```
[ 7 7 10 9 8]
[ 6 10 2 5 9]
[ 2 9 2 10 2]
[9 6 3 2 1]
```

To traverse through all the items in the two-dimensional array, you can use the nested foreach loop, as follows:

Script 24:

```
for rows ininteger_random:
for column in rows:
print(column)
```

Output:

```
7
7
10
9
8
6
10
2
5
9
2
9
2
10
2
9
6
3
2
1
```

In the next section, you will see how to add, remove, and sort elements in a NumPy array.

2.5. Adding Items in a NumPy Array

To add the items into a NumPy array, you can use the append() method from the NumPy module. First, you need to pass the original array and the item that you want to append to the array to the append() method. The append() method returns a new array that contains newly added items appended to the end of the original array.

The following script adds a text item "Yellow" to an existing array with three items.

Script 25:

```
importnumpyasnp

my_array = np.array(["Red", "Green", "Orange"])
print(my_array)

extended = np.append(my_array, "Yellow")
print(extended)
```

Output:

```
['Red' 'Green' 'Orange']
['Red' 'Green' 'Orange' 'Yellow']
```

In addition to adding one item at a time, you can also append an array of items to an existing array. The method remains similar to appending a single item. You just have to pass the existing array and the new array to the append() method, which returns a concatenated array where items from the new array are appended at the end of the original array.

Script 26:

```
importnumpyasnp

my_array = np.array(["Red", "Green", "Orange"])
print(my_array)

extended = np.append(my_array, ["Yellow", "Pink"])
print(extended)
```

Output:

```
['Red' 'Green' 'Orange']
['Red' 'Green' 'Orange' 'Yellow' 'Pink']
```

To add items in a two-dimensional NumPy array, you have to specify whether you want to add the new item as a row or as a column. To do so, you can take the help of the axis attribute of the append method.

Let's first create a 3 x 3 array of all zeros.

Script 27:

```
zeros_array = np.zeros((3,3))
print(zeros_array)
```

The output shows all the rows from our two-dimensional NumPy array.

Output:

```
[[0. 0. 0.]
 [0. 0. 0.]
 [0. 0. 0.]]
```

To add a new row in the above 3 x 3 array, you need to pass the original array to the new array in the form of a row vector and the axis attribute to the append() method. To add a new array in the form of a row, you need to set 0 as the value for the axis attribute.

Here is an example script.

Script 28:

```
zeros_array = np.zeros((3,3))
print(zeros_array)
print("Extended Array")
extended = np.append(zeros_array, [[1, 2, 3]], axis = 0)
print(extended)
```

In the output below, you can see that a new row has been appended to our original 3 x 3 array of all zeros.

Output:

```
[[0. 0. 0.]
 [0. 0. 0.]
 [0. 0. 0.]]
Extended Array
[[0. 0. 0.]
 [0. 0. 0.]
 [0. 0. 0.]
 [1. 2. 3.]]
```

To append a new array as a column in the existing 2-D array, you need to set the value of the axis attribute to 1.

Script 29:

```
zeros_array = np.zeros((3,3))
print(zeros_array)
print("Extended Array")
extended = np.append(zeros_array, [[1],[2],[3]], axis = 1)
print(extended)
```

Output:

```
[[0. 0. 0.]
 [0. 0. 0.]
 [0. 0. 0.]]
Extended Array
[[0. 0. 0. 1.]
 [0. 0. 0. 2.]
 [0. 0. 0. 3.]]
```

2.6. Removing Items from a NumPy Array

To delete an item from an array, you may use the delete() method. You need to pass the existing array and the index of the item to be deleted to the delete() method. The following script deletes an item at index 1 (second item) from the my_array array.

Script 30:

```
importnumpyasnp

my_array = np.array(["Red", "Green", "Orange"])
print(my_array)

print("After deletion")
updated_array = np.delete(my_array, 1)
print(updated_array)
```

The output shows that the item at index 1, i.e., "Green," is deleted.

Output:

```
['Red' 'Green' 'Orange']
After deletion
['Red' 'Orange']
```

If you want to delete multiple items from an array, you can pass the item indexes in the form of a list to the delete() method. For example, the following script deletes the items at index 1 and 2 from the NumPy array named my_array.

Script 31:

```
importnumpyasnp

my_array = np.array(["Red", "Green", "Orange"])
print(my_array)

print("After deletion")
updated_array = np.delete(my_array, [1,2])
print(updated_array)
```

Output:

```
['Red' 'Green' 'Orange']
After deletion
['Red']
```

You can delete a row or column from a 2-D array using the delete method. However, just as you did with the append() method for adding items, you need to specify whether you want to delete a row or column using the axis attribute.

The following script creates an integer array with four rows and five columns. Next, the delete() method is used to delete the row at index 1 (second row). Notice here that to delete the array, the value of the axis attribute is set to 0.

Script 32:

```
integer_random = np.random.randint(1,11, size=(4, 5))
print(integer_random)

print("After deletion")
updated_array = np.delete(integer_random, 1, axis = 0)
print(updated_array)
```

The output shows that the second row is deleted from the input 2-D array.

Output:

```
[[ 2 3 3 3 4]
[ 1 7 6 7 10]
[ 7 1 6 6 8]
[ 3 7 8 10 7]]
Afterdeletion
[[ 2 3 3 3 4]
[ 7 1 6 6 8]
[ 3 7 8 10 7]]
```

Finally, to delete a column, you can set the value of the axis attribute to 1, as shown below:

Script 33:

```
integer_random = np.random.randint(1,11, size=(4, 5))
print(integer_random)

print("After deletion")
updated_array = np.delete(integer_random, 1, axis = 1)
print(updated_array)
```

The output shows all the rows from our two-dimensional NumPy array.

Output:

```
[[ 9 10 10 5 5]
[ 5 1 2 4 2]
[ 5 1 3 7 8]
[ 5 1 8 2 5]]
Afterdeletion
[[ 9 10 5 5]
[ 5 2 4 2]
[ 5 3 7 8]
[ 5 8 2 5]]
```

Further Readings - Basics of NumPy

Check the official documentation here (https://bit.ly/3oJRxE3) to learn more about NumPy.

Hands-on Time - Exercise

Now, it is your turn. Follow the instructions in **the exercises below** to check your understanding of basic NumPy operations. The answers to these questions are given at the end of the book.

Exercise 2.1

Question 1:

To generate an identity matrix of four rows and four columns, which of the following functions can be used?

A. np.identity(4,4)

B. np.id(4,4)

C. np.eye(4,4)

D. All of the above

Question 2:

To delete a column from a two-dimensional NumPy array, the value of the axis attribute of the delete method should be set to:

A. 0

B. 1

C. column_number

D. All of the above

Question 3:

How to create the array of numbers 4,7,10,13,16 with NumPy?

A. np.arange(3, 16, 3)

B. np.arange(4, 16, 3)

C. np.arange(4, 15,3)

D. None of the above

Exercise 2.2

Create a random NumPy array of five rows and four columns.

3

NumPy Array Manipulation

In this chapter, you will learn about some of the most common array manipulation functions in NumPy. So, let's begin without much ado.

3.1. Sorting NumPy Arrays

You can sort NumPy arrays of various types. Numeric arrays are sorted by default in ascending order of numbers. On the other hand, text arrays are sorted alphabetically.

3.1.1. Sorting Numeric Arrays

To sort an array in NumPy, you may call the np.sort() function and pass it to your NumPy array. The following script shows how to sort a NumPy array of 10 random integers between 1 and 20.

Script 1:

```
importnumpyasnp

print("unsorted array")
my_array = np.random.randint(1,20,10)
print(my_array)
```

```
print("\nsorted array")
sorted_array = np.sort(my_array)
print(sorted_array)
```

Output:

```
unsortedarray
[17 9 5 2 12 16 8 12 12 7]

sortedarray
[ 2 5 7 8 9 12 12 12 16 17]
```

3.1.2. Sorting Text Arrays

As mentioned earlier, text arrays are sorted in alphabetical order. Here is an example of how you can sort a text array with the NumPy sort() method.

Script 2:

```
importnumpyasnp

print("unsorted array")
my_array = np.array(["Red", "Green", "Blue", "Yello"])
print(my_array)

print("\nsorted array")
sorted_array = np.sort(my_array)
print(sorted_array)
```

Output:

```
unsorted array
['Red' 'Green' 'Blue' 'Yello']

sorted array
['Blue' 'Green' 'Red' 'Yello']
```

3.1.3. Sorting Boolean Arrays

Finally, Boolean arrays are sorted in a way that all the False values appear first in an array. Here is an example of how you can sort the Boolean arrays in NumPy.

Script 3:

```
importnumpyasnp

print("unsorted array")
my_array = np.array([False, True, True, False, False, True,
False, True])
print(my_array)

print("\nSorted array")
sorted_array = np.sort(my_array)
print(sorted_array)
```

Output:

```
unsorted array
[False TrueTrue False False True False True]

Sorted array
[False FalseFalseFalse TrueTrueTrue True]
```

3.1.4. Sorting 2-D Arrays

NumPy also allows you to sort two-dimensional arrays. In two-dimensional arrays, each item itself is an array. The sort() function sorts an item in each individual array in a two-dimensional array.

The script below creates a two-dimensional array of shape (4,6) containing random integers between 1 to 20. The array is then sorted via the np.sort() method.

Script 4:

```
importnumpyasnp

print("unsorted array")
my_array = np.random.randint(1,20, size = (4,6))
print(my_array)

print("\Sorted array")
sorted_array = np.sort(my_array)
print(sorted_array)
```

Output:

```
unsortedarray
[[12 2 8 5 1 14]
[ 6 17 7 13 6 4]
[ 5 6 6 2 6 19]
[ 2 12 14 12 4 9]]
Sortedarray
[[ 1 2 5 8 12 14]
[ 4 6 6 7 13 17]
[ 2 5 6 6 6 19]
[ 2 4 9 12 12 14]]
```

3.1.5. Sorting in Descending Order

You can also sort an array in descending order. To do so, you can first sort an array in ascending order via the sort() method. Next, you can pass the sorted array to the flipud() method, which reverses the sorted array and returns the array sorted in descending order. Here is an example of how you can sort an array in descending order.

Script 5:

```
importnumpyasnp

print("unsorted array")
my_array = np.random.randint(1,20,10)
print(my_array)

print("\nsorted array")
sorted_array = np.sort(my_array)
reverse_sorted = np.flipud(sorted_array)
print(reverse_sorted)
```

Output:

```
unsortedarray
[15 18 16 3 2 1 4 16 2 3]

sortedarray
[18 16 16 15 4 3 3 2 2 1]
```

3.2. Reshaping NumPy Arrays

You can also modify the shape of a NumPy array. To do so, you can use the reshape() method and pass it the new shape for your NumPy array.

In this section, you will see how to reshape a NumPy array from lower to higher dimensions and vice versa.

3.2.1. Reshaping from Lower to Higher Dimensions

The following script defines a one-dimensional array of 10 random integers between 1 and 20. The reshape() function reshapes the array into the shape (2,5).

Script 6:

```
importnumpyasnp

print("one-dimensional array")
one_d_array = np.random.randint(1,20,10)
print(one_d_array)

print("\ntwo-dimensional array")
two_d_array = one_d_array.reshape(2,5)
print(two_d_array)
```

Output:

```
one-dimensional array
[ 4 14 12 17 18 17 2 19 18 11]

two-dimensional array
[[ 4 14 12 17 18]
 [17 2 19 18 11]]
```

It is important to mention that the product of the rows and columns of the original array must match the value of the product of rows and columns of the reshaped array. For instance, the shape of the original array in the last script was (10,) with product 10. The product of the rows and columns in the reshaped array was also 10 (2 x 5)

You can also call the reshape() function directly from the NumPy module and pass it the array to be reshaped as the first argument and the shape tuple as the second argument. Here is an example which converts an array of shape (10,) to (2,5).

Script 7:

```
importnumpyasnp

print("one-dimensional array")
one_d_array = np.random.randint(1,20,10)
print(one_d_array)

print("\ntwo-dimensional array")
two_d_array = np.reshape(one_d_array,(2,5))
print(two_d_array)
```

Output:

```
one-dimensional array
[ 9 17 19 16 8 15 6 6 13 17]

two-dimensional array
[[ 9 17 19 16 8]
 [15 6 6 13 17]]
```

Let's see another example of reshaping a NumPy array from lower to higher dimensions.

The following script defines a NumPy array of shape (4,6). The original array is then reshaped to a three-dimensional array of shape (3, 4, 2). Notice here again that the product of dimensions of the original array (4 x 6) and the reshaped array (3 x 4 x 2) is the same, i.e., 24.

Script 8:

```
importnumpyasnp

print("two-dimensional array")
two_d_array = np.random.randint(1,20, size = (4,6))
print(one_d_array)

print("\nthree-dimensional array")
three_d_array = np.reshape(two_d_array,(3,4,2))
print(two_d_array)
```

Output:

```
two-dimensional array
[ 9 17 19 16 8 15 6 6 13 17]

three-dimensional array
[[17 17 3 11 9 5]
[ 6 18 7 5 14 7]
 [14 5 4 9 11 1]
 [16 8 9 7 16 16]]
```

Let's try to reshape a NumPy array in a way that the product of dimensions does not match.

In the script below, the shape of the original array is (4,6). Next, you try to reshape this array to the shape (1,4,2). In this case, since the product of dimensions of the original and the reshaped array don't match, you will see an error in the output.

Script 9:

```
importnumpyasnp

print("two-dimensional array")
two_d_array = np.random.randint(1,20, size = (4,6))
print(one_d_array)

print("\nthree-dimensional array")
three_d_array = np.reshape(two_d_array,(1,4,2))
print(two_d_array)
```

Output:

```
ValueError: cannot reshape array of size 24 into shape (1,4,2)
```

3.2.2. Reshaping from Higher to Lower Dimensions

Let's now see a few examples of reshaping NumPy arrays from higher to lower dimensions.

In the script below, the original array is of shape (4,6) while the new array is of shape (24). The reshaping, in this case, will be successful since the product of dimensions for original and reshaped arrays is the same.

Script 10:

```
importnumpyasnp

print("two-dimensional array")
two_d_array = np.random.randint(1,20, size = (4,6))
print(two_d_array)

print("\none-dimensional array")
one_d_array = two_d_array.reshape(24)
print(one_d_array)
```

Output:

```
two-dimensional array
[[ 6  6 15  3 11 14]
 [14  4  8 17 10  6]
 [ 5 14  3  5 15 14]
 [12  3 15 15  5 16]]

one-dimensional array
[ 6  6 15  3 11 14 14  4  8 17 10  6  5 14  3  5 15 14 12  3 15 15  5
   16]
```

Finally, to convert an array of any dimensions to a flat, one-dimensional array, you will need to pass −1 as the argument for the reshaped function, as shown in the script below, which converts a two-dimensional array to a one-dimensional array.

Script 11:

```
importnumpyasnp

print("two-dimensional array")
two_d_array = np.random.randint(1,20, size = (4,6))
print(two_d_array)

print("\none-dimensional array")
one_d_array = two_d_array.reshape(-1)
print(one_d_array)
```

Output:

```
two-dimensional array
[[ 5 10 10 11 18 12]
 [12 3 4 7 5 2]
 [ 5 11 3 6 19 9]
 [16 2 7 6 4 4]]

one-dimensional array
[ 5 10 10 11 18 12 12 3 4 7 5 2 5 11 3 6 19 9 16 2 7 6 4 4]
```

Similarly, the following script converts a three-dimensional array to a one-dimensional array.

Script 12:

```
importnumpyasnp

print("two-dimensional array")
three_d_array = np.random.randint(1,20, size = (4,2,6))
print(three_d_array )

print("\non-dimensional array")
one_d_array = three_d_array .reshape(-1)
print(one_d_array)
```

Output:

```
two-dimensionalarray
[[[14 2 2 18 19 4]
  [16 3 14 6 5 15]]

[[ 3 16 10 14 14 8]
  [12 15 1 5 16 11]]

[[ 9 5 1 12 13 8]
[ 5 11 18 10 19 5]]

  [[13 1 8 6 19 3]
  [19 1 6 15 12 3]]]

one-dimensionalarray
[14 2 2 18 19 4 16 3 14 6 5 15 3 16 10 14 14 8 12 15 1 5 16 11
9 5 1 12 13 8 5 11 18 10 19 5 13 1 8 6 19 3 19 1 6 15 12 3]
```

3.3. Indexing and Slicing NumPy Arrays

NumPy arrays can be indexed and sliced. Slicing an array means dividing an array into multiple parts.

NumPy arrays are indexed just like normal lists. Indexes in NumPy arrays start from 0, which means that the first item of a NumPy array is stored at the 0th index.

The following script creates a simple NumPy array of the first 10 positive integers.

Script 13:

```
importnumpyasnp
s = np.arange(1,11)
print(s)
```

Output:

```
[ 1 2 3 4 5 6 7 8 9 10]
```

The item at index one can be accessed as follows:

Script 14:

```
print(s[1])
```

Output:

```
2
```

To slice an array, you have to pass the lower index, followed by a colon and the upper index. The items from the lower index (inclusive) to the upper index (exclusive) will be filtered. The following script slices the array "s" from the 1st index to the 9th index. The elements from index 1 to 8 are printed in the output.

Script 15:

```
print(s[1:9])
```

Output:

```
[2 3 4 5 6 7 8 9]
```

If you specify only the upper bound, all the items from the first index to the upper bound are returned. Similarly, if you specify only the lower bound, all the items from the lower bound to the last item of the array are returned.

Script 16:

```
print(s[:5])
print(s[5:])
```

Output:

```
[1 2 3 4 5]
[ 6 7 8 9 10]
```

Array slicing can also be applied on a two-dimensional array. To do so, you have to apply slicing on arrays and columns separately. A comma separates the rows and columns slicing.

In the following script, the rows from the first and second indexes are returned, while all the columns are returned. You can see the first two complete rows in the output.

Script 17:

```
row1 = [10,12,13]
row2 = [45,32,16]
row3 = [45,32,16]

nums_2d = np.array([row1, row2, row3])
print(nums_2d[:2,:])
```

Output:

```
[[10 12 13]
 [45 32 16]]
```

Similarly, the following script returns all the rows but only the first two columns.

Script 18:

```
row1 = [10,12,13]
row2 = [45,32,16]
row3 = [45,32,16]

nums_2d = np.array([row1, row2, row3])

print(nums_2d[:,:2])
```

Output:

```
[[10 12]
 [45 32]
 [45 32]]
```

Let's see another example of slicing. Here, we will slice the rows from row one to the end of rows and column one to the end of columns. (Remember, row and column numbers start from 0.) In the output, you will see the last two rows and the last two columns.

Script 19:

```
row1 = [10,12,13]
row2 = [45,32,16]
row3 = [45,32,16]

nums_2d = np.array([row1, row2, row3])
print(nums_2d[1:,1:])
```

Output:

```
[[32 16]
 [32 16]]
```

3.4. Broadcasting NumPy Arrays

Broadcasting allows you to perform various operations between NumPy arrays of different shapes. This is best explained with the help of an example.

In the script below, you define two arrays: a one-dimensional array of three items and another scaler array that contains only one item. Next, the two arrays are added. Finally, in the output, you will see that the scaler value, i.e., 10 is added to all the items in the array that contains three items. This is an amazing ability and is extremely useful in many scenarios, such as machine learning and artificial neural networks.

Script 20:

```
importnumpyasnp

array1 = np.array ([14,25,31])
array2 = np.array([10])
result = array1 + array2
print(result)
```

Output:

```
[24 35 41]
```

Let's see another example of broadcasting. In the script below, you add a two-dimensional array with three rows and four columns to a scaler array with one item. In the output, you will see that the scaler value, i.e., 10, will be added to all the 12 items in the first array, which contains three rows and four columns.

Script 21:

```
array1 = np.random.randint(1,20, size = (3,4))
print(array1)

array2 = np.array([10])

print("after bradcasting")
result = array1 + array2
print(result)
```

Output:

```
[[ 2 11 16 19]
 [14 15 13 19]
[ 9 6 18 4]]
afterbradcasting
[[12 21 26 29]
 [24 25 23 29]
 [19 16 28 14]]
```

You can also use broadcasting to perform operations between two-dimensional and one-dimensional arrays.

For example, the following script creates two arrays: a two-dimensional array of three rows and four columns and a one-dimensional array of one row and four columns. If you perform addition between these two rows, you will see that the values in a one-dimensional array will be added to the corresponding columns' values in all the rows in the two-dimensional array.

For instance, the first row in the two-dimensional array contains values 4, 6, 1, and 2. When you add the one-dimensional array with values 5, 10, 20, and 25 to it, the first row of the two-dimensional array becomes 9, 16, 21, and 27.

Script 22:

```
array1 = np.random.randint(1,20, size = (3,4))
print(array1)

array2 = np.array([5,10,20,25])

print("after bradcasting")
result = array1 + array2
print(result)
```

Output:

```
[[ 4 6 1 2]
 [19 2 16 7]
 [19 7 19 6]]
afterbradcasting
[[ 9 16 21 27]
 [24 12 36 32]
 [24 17 39 31]]
```

Finally, let's see an example where an array with three rows and one column is added to another array with three rows and four columns. Since, in this case, the values of row match, therefore, in the output, for each column in the two-dimensional array, the values from the one- dimensional array are added row-wise. For instance, the first column in the two-dimensional array contains the values 10, 19, and 11. When you add the one-dimensional array (5, 10, 20) to it, the new column value becomes 15, 29, and 31.

Script 23:

```
array1 = np.random.randint(1,20, size = (3,4))
print(array1)

array2 = np.array([[5],[10],[20]])

print("after bradcasting")
result = array1 + array2
print(result)
```

Output:

```
[[10 17 7 3]
 [19 9 14 17]
 [11 15 11 10]]
afterbradcasting
[[15 22 12 8]
 [29 19 24 27]
 [31 35 31 30]]
```

3.5. Copying NumPy Arrays

There are two main ways to copy an array in NumPy. You can either copy the contents of the original array, or you can copy the reference to the original array into another array.

To copy the contents of the original array into a new array, you can call the copy() function on the original array. Now, if you modify the contents of the new array, the contents of the original array are not modified.

For instance, in the script below, in the copied array2, the item at index 1 is updated. However, when you print the original array, you see that the index one for the original array is not modified.

Script 24:

```
importnumpyasnp
array1 = np.array([10,12,14,16,18,20])

array2 = array1.copy()
array2[1] = 20

print(array1)
print(array2)
```

Output:

```
[10 12 14 16 18 20]
[10 20 14 16 18 20]
```

The other method to copy an array in Python is via the view() method. However, with the view method, if the contents of a new array are modified, the original array is also modified. Here is an example:

Script 25:

```
array1 = np.array([10,12,14,16,18,20])

array2 = array1.view()
array2[1] = 20

print(array1)
print(array2)
```

Output:

```
[10 20 14 16 18 20]
[10 20 14 16 18 20]
```

3.6. NumPy I/O Operations

You can save and load NumPy arrays to and from your local drive.

3.6.1. Saving a NumPy Array

To save a NumPy array, you need to call the save() method from the NumPy module and pass it the file name for your NumPy as the first argument, while the array object itself as the second argument. Here is an example:

Script 26:

```
importnumpyasnp
array1 = np.array([10,12,14,16,18,20])

np.save("D:\Datasets\my_array", array1)
```

The save() method saves a NumPy array in "NPY" file format. You can also

save a NumPy array in the form of a text file, as shown in the following script:

Script 27:

```
importnumpyasnp
array1 = np.array([10,12,14,16,18,20])

np.savetxt("D:\Datasets\my_array.txt", array1)
```

3.6.2. Loading a NumPy Array

To load a NumPy array in the "NPY" format, you can use the load() method, as shown in the following example.

Script 28:

```
importnumpyasnp
loaded_array = np.load("D:\Datasets\my_array.npy")
print(loaded_array)
```

Output:

```
[10 12 14 16 18 20]
```

On the other hand, if your NumPy array is stored in the text form, you may use the loadtxt() method to load such a NumPy array.

Script 29:

```
importnumpyasnp
loaded_array = np.loadtxt("D:\Datasets\my_array.txt")
print(loaded_array)
```

Output:

```
[10. 12. 14. 16. 18. 20.]
```

Further Readings – Basics of NumPy

Check the official documentation here (https://bit.ly/3oJRxE3) to learn more about NumPy.

Hands-on Time – Exercise

Now, it is your turn. Follow the instructions in **the exercises below** to check your understanding of the basics of NumPy array manipulation. The answers to these questions are given at the end of the book.

Exercise 3.1

Question 1:

Which function is used to convert a multi-dimensional NumPy array into a flat array of 1-dimension?

A. np.reshape(0)

B. np.reshape(-1)

C. np.reshape(1)

D. None of the Above

Question 2:

Which function is used to save a NumPy array in text format?

A. np.savetext()

B. np.saveText()

C. np.saveTxt()

D. np.savetxt()

Question 3:

To sort a NumPy array in descending order, you can use the following function:

A. np.flipud(np.sort(my_array))

B. np.sort(np.flip(my_array))

C. np.sort()

D. np.flip()

Exercise 3.2

Create a random NumPy array of 4 rows and 5 columns. Then, using array indexing and slicing, display the items from row 3 to end and column 2 to end.

4

NumPy Tips and Tricks

In the previous chapter, you saw some of the most common ways to manipulate NumPy arrays. In this chapter, you will be introduced to a few common tips and tricks that will come in handy while working with NumPy arrays.

4.1. Statistical Operations with NumPy

NumPy arrays contain various functionalities for performing statistical operations, such as finding the mean, median, and standard deviations of items in a NumPy array.

4.1.1. Finding the Mean

To find the mean or average of all the items in a NumPy array, you need to pass the array to the mean() method of the NumPy module. Here is an example:

Script 1:

```
importnumpyasnp

my_array = np.array([2,4,8,10,12])
print(my_array)
print("mean:")
print(np.mean(my_array))
```

Output:

```
[ 2 4 8 10 12]
mean:
7.2
```

You can also find the mean in a two-dimensional NumPy array across rows and columns. To find the mean across columns, you need to pass 1 as the value for the axis parameter of the mean method. Similarly, to find the mean across rows, you need to pass 0 as the parameter value.

The following script finds the mean of a two-dimensional array containing two rows and three columns across rows and columns.

Script 2:

```
importnumpyasnp

my_array = np.random.randint(1,20, size = (2,3))
print(my_array)
print("mean:")
print(np.mean(my_array, axis = 1))
print(np.mean(my_array, axis = 0))
```

Output:

```
[[10 13 18]
 [19 18 1]]
mean:
[13.66666667 12.66666667]
[14.5 15.5 9.5]
```

4.1.2. Finding the Median

The median() method from the NumPy module is used to find the median value in a NumPy array. Here is an example.

Script 3:

```
importnumpyasnp

my_array = np.array([2,4,8,10,12])
print(my_array)
print("median:")
print(np.median(my_array))
```

Output:

```
[ 2 4 8 10 12]
median:
8.0
```

Similarly, to find the median values across columns and rows in a two-dimensional array, you need to pass 1 and 0, respectively, as the values for the axis attribute of the median method.

The following script finds the median values across rows and columns for a two-dimensional array with three rows and five columns.

Script 4:

```
importnumpyasnp

my_array = np.random.randint(1,20, size = (3,5))
print(my_array)
print("median:")
print(np.median(my_array, axis = 1))
print(np.median(my_array, axis = 0))
```

Output:

```
[[18 15 8 15 17]
[ 8 8 5 4 9]
 [11 12 14 2 6]]
median:
[15. 8. 11.]
[11. 12. 8. 4. 9.]
```

4.1.3. Finding the Max and Min Values

The max() function returns the maximum value from the array, while the min() function returns the minimum value.

The following script returns the minimum value in a NumPy array using the min() method.

Script 5:

```
importnumpyasnp

my_array = np.array([2,4,8,10,12])
print(my_array)
print("min value:")
print(np.amin(my_array))
```

Output:

```
[ 2 4 8 10 12]
min value:
2
```

You can get the minimum values across all rows or columns in a two-dimensional NumPy array by passing 0 or 1 as values for the axis attribute of the min() method. The value of 1 for the axis attribute returns the minimum values across all columns, whereas a value of 0 returns the minimum values across all rows.

Script 6:

```
importnumpyasnp

my_array = np.random.randint(1,20, size = (3,4))
print(my_array)
print("min:")
print(np.amin(my_array, axis = 1))
print(np.amin(my_array, axis = 0))
```

Output:

```
[[15 7 18 6]
 [13 15 19 13]
[ 1 11 17 2]]
min:
[ 6 13 1]
[ 1 7 17 2]
```

To get the maximum value from a NumPy array, you may use the max() method, as shown in the script below:

Script 7:

```
importnumpyasnp

my_array = np.array([2,4,8,10,12])
print(my_array)
print("max value:")
print(np.amax(my_array))
```

Output:

```
[ 2 4 8 10 12]
max value:
12
```

Like the min() method, which returns the minimum value, you can get the maximum values across all rows or columns in a two-dimensional NumPy array by passing 0 or 1 as values for the axis attribute of the max() method. The value of 1 for the axis attribute returns the minimum values across all columns, whereas a value of 0 returns the minimum values across all rows.

Script 8:

```
importnumpyasnp

my_array = np.random.randint(1,20, size = (3,4))
print(my_array)
print("max:")
print(np.amax(my_array, axis = 1))
print(np.amax(my_array, axis = 0))
```

Output:

```
[[17 14 9 7]
[ 9 11 18 2]
 [18 12 14 16]]
max:
[17 18 18]
[18 14 18 16]
```

4.1.4. Finding Standard Deviation

The standard deviation of a NumPy array can be found via the std() method.

Here is an example:

Script 9:

```
importnumpyasnp

my_array = np.array([2,4,8,10,12])
print(my_array)
print("std value:")
print(np.std(my_array))
```

Output:

```
[ 2 4 8 10 12]
std value:
3.7094473981982814
```

To find the standard deviation across rows and columns in a two-dimensional NumPy array, you need to call the std() method. The value of 1 for the axis attribute returns the minimum list of minimum values across all columns, whereas a value of 0 returns minimum values across all rows.

Script 10:

```
importnumpyasnp

my_array = np.random.randint(1,20, size = (3,4))
print(my_array)
print("std-dev:")
print(np.std(my_array, axis = 1))
print(np.std(my_array, axis = 0))
```

Output:

```
[[16 13 16 8]
[ 5 12 2 6]
 [14 12 4 11]]
std-dev:
[3.26917421 3.63145976 3.76662979]
[4.78423336 0.47140452 6.18241233 2.05480467]
```

4.1.5. Finding Correlations

Finally, to find correlations, you can use the correlation() method and pass it the two NumPy arrays between which you want to find the correlation.

Script 11:

```
importnumpyasnp

a1 = np.array([1, 3, 0, 0.9, 1.2])
a2 = np.array([-1, 0.5, 0.2, 0.6, 5])

print(a1)
print(a2)
```

```
print(«correlation value:»)
print(np.correlate(a1, a2))
```

Output:

```
[1. 3. 0. 0.9 1.2]
[-1.  0.5 0.2 0.6 5. ]
correlation value:
[7.04]
```

4.2. Getting Unique Items and Counts

Oftentimes, you would need to find unique values within a NumPy array and to find the count of every unique value in a NumPy array.

To find unique values in a NumPy array, you need to pass the array to the unique() method from the NumPy module. Here is an example:

Script 12:

```
importnumpyasnp

my_array =np.array([5,8,7,5,9,3,7,7,1,1,8,4,6,9,7,3])
unique_items = np.unique(my_array )

print(unique_items)
```

Output:

```
[1 3 4 5 6 7 8 9]
```

To find the count of every unique item in a NumPy array, you need to pass the array to the unique() method and pass True as the value for the return_counts attribute. The unique() method in this case returns a tuple, which contains a list of all unique items and a corresponding list of counts for each unique item. Here is an example:

Script 13:

```
importnumpyasnp

my_array =np.array([5,8,7,5,9,3,7,7,1,1,8,4,6,9,7,3])
unique_items, counts = np.unique(my_array, return_counts=True)

print(unique_items)
print(counts)
```

Output:

```
[1 3 4 5 6 7 8 9]
[2 2 1 2 1 4 2 2]
```

One way to get the count value against every unique item is to create an array of arrays where the first item is the list of unique items and the second item is the list of counts, as shown in the script below:

Script 14:

```
frequencies = np.asarray((unique_items, counts))
print(frequencies)
```

Output:

```
[[1 3 4 5 6 7 8 9]
 [2 2 1 2 1 4 2 2]]
```

Next, you can transpose the array that contains the list of unique items and their counts. In the output, you will get an array where each item is a list. The first item in the list is the unique item itself, while the second is the count of the item. For instance, in the output of the script below, you can see that item 1 occurs twice in the input array, item 3 also occurs twice, and so on.

Script 15:

```
frequencies = np.asarray((unique_items, counts)).T
print(frequencies)
```

Output:

```
[[1 2]
 [3 2]
 [4 1]
 [5 2]
 [6 1]
 [7 4]
 [8 2]
 [9 2]]
```

4.3. Reversing a NumPy Array

There are two main methods to reverse a NumPy array: flipud() and fliplr(). The flipud() method is used to reverse a one-dimensional NumPy array, as shown in the script below:

Script 16:

```
importnumpyasnp

print("original")
my_array = np.random.randint(1,20,10)
print(my_array)

print("reversed")
reversed_array = np.flipud(my_array)
print(reversed_array)
```

Output:

```
original
[ 2 12 7 1 6 7 18 14 2 1]
reversed
[ 1 2 14 18 7 6 1 7 12 2]
```

On the other hand, to reverse a two-dimensional NumPy array, you can use the fliplr() method, as shown below:

Script 17:

```
importnumpyasnp

print("original")
my_array = np.random.randint(1,20, size = (3,4))
print(my_array)

print("reversed")
reversed_array = np.fliplr(my_array)
print(reversed_array)
```

Output:

```
original
[[10 3 4 3]
 [14 13 18 19]
[ 2 5 11 1]]
reversed
[[ 3 4 3 10]
 [19 18 13 14]
[ 1 11 5 2]]
```

4.4. Importing and Exporting CSV Files

CSV files are an important source of data. The NumPy library contains functions that allow you to store NumPy arrays in the form of CSV files. The NumPy module also allows you to load CSV files into NumPy arrays.

4.4.1. Saving a NumPy File as CSV

To save a NumPy array in the form of a CSV file, you can use the tofile() method and pass it your NumPy array.

The following script stores a two-dimensional array of three rows and four columns to a CSV file. You can see that you need to pass a comma "," as the value for the sep parameter.

Script 18:

```
importnumpyasnp

my_array = np.random.randint(1,20, size = (3,4))
print(my_array)

my_array.tofile('D:\Datasets\my_array.csv', sep = ',')
```

The following NumPy array will be stored in the form of a CSV file.

Output:

```
[[ 4 17 8 14]
[ 9 18 4 4]
[ 8 6 7 2]]
```

If you open the CSV file, you will see the following data:

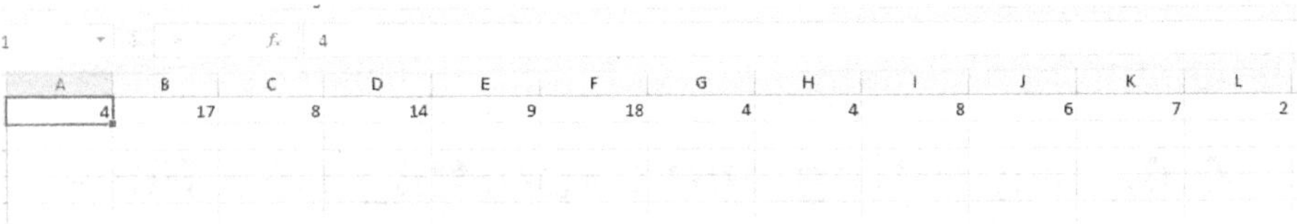

You can see from the above output that though the NumPy array you stored had two dimensions, it is flattened and stored as a single row in your CSV file. This is the default behavior of the tofile() function.

To store a two-dimensional NumPy array in the form of multiple rows in a CSV file, you can use the savetxt() method from the NumPy module, as shown in the following script.

Script 19:

```
importnumpyasnp

my_array = np.random.randint(1,20, size = (3,4))
print(my_array)

np.savetxt('D:\Datasets\my_array2.csv', my_array, delimiter =
    ",")
```

Output:

```
[[ 5 2 5 4]
 [16 3 3 16]
 [19 10 15 1]]
```

If you open your newly created CSV file now, you should see the following information:

A	B	C	D
5.00E+00	2.00E+00	5.00E+00	4.00E+00
1.60E+01	3.00E+00	3.00E+00	1.60E+01
1.90E+01	1.00E+01	1.50E+01	1.00E+00

4.4.2. Loading CSV Files into NumPy Arrays

To load a CSV file into a NumPy array, you can use the genfromtxt() method and pass it the CSV file along with a comma "," as the value for the delimiter attribute of the genfromtxt() method. Here is an example:

Script 20:

```
importnumpyasnp

loaded_array = np.genfromtxt('D:\Datasets\my_array2.csv',
    delimiter=',')
print(loaded_array)
```

Output:

```
[[ 5. 2. 5. 4.]
 [16. 3. 3. 16.]
 [19. 10. 15. 1.]]
```

4.5. Plotting NumPy Arrays with Matplotlib

You can use NumPy arrays along with Matplotlib plotting functionalities to plot various types of graphs. You will see some examples in this section.

The following script creates two NumPy arrays. The first array contains 20 equidistant numbers between 0 and 20, and the second array contains the square of these values. Next, the plot() method from the pyplot module of the Matplotlib library is used to plot a line plot using the two input arrays.

Script 21:

```
importnumpyasnp
importmatplotlib.pyplotasplt
%matplotlib inline

importmatplotlib.pyplotasplt
importnumpyasnp
importmath

x_vals = np.linspace(0, 20, 20)
print(x_vals)
y_vals = [math.sqrt(i) foriinx_vals]
plt.plot(x_vals, y_vals)
```

Output:

```
[ 0.         1.05263158 2.10526316 3.15789474 4.21052632
   5.26315789 6.31578947 7.36842105 8.42105263 9.47368421
   10.52631579 11.57894737  12.63157895 13.68421053
   14.73684211 15.78947368 16.84210526 17.89473684
   18.94736842 20.        ]
```

```
[<matplotlib.lines.Line2D at 0x1be2a784550>]
```

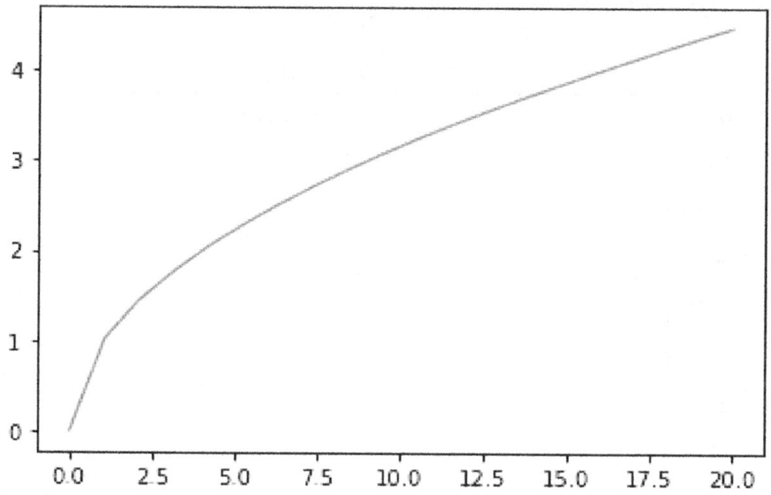

Similarly, you can draw graphs using multiple NumPy arrays. The following script plots a line plot that displays squares and cubes of 20 equidistant numbers between 0 and 20.

Script 22:

```
importmatplotlib.pyplotasplt
importnumpyasnp
importmath


x_vals = np.linspace(0, 20, 20)
y_vals = [math.sqrt(i) foriinx_vals]
y2_vals = x_vals ** 3
plt.xlabel('X Values')
plt.ylabel('Y Values')
plt.title('Square Roots')
plt.plot(x_vals, y_vals, 'r', label = 'Square Root')
plt.plot(x_vals, y2_vals, 'b', label = 'Cube')
plt.legend(loc='upper center')
```

Output:

```
<matplotlib.legend.Legend at 0x1be2c83ee50>
```

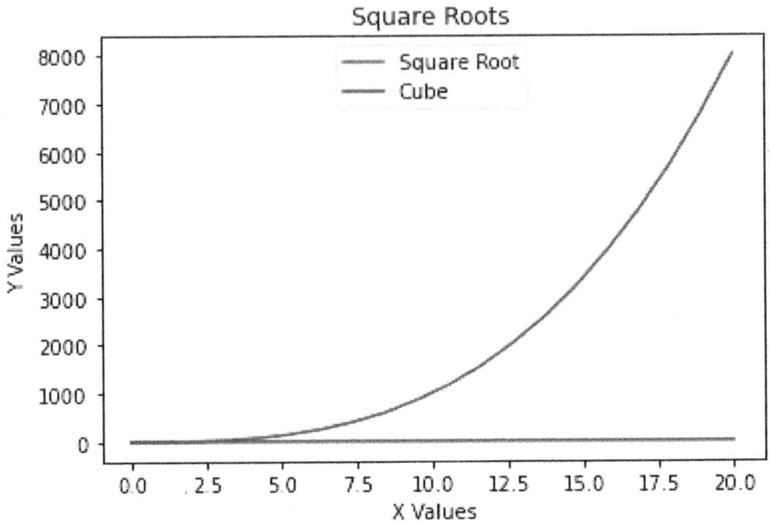

Finally, you can also plot heatmaps using a two-dimensional NumPy array by passing the array to the imshow() method of the pyplot module of the Matplotlib library.

Script 23:

```
importnumpyasnp
importmatplotlib.pyplotasplt

my_array = np.random.randint(1,20, size = (4,4))
print(my_array)

plt.imshow(my_array)
plt.show()
```

Output:

```
[[ 7 19 12 1]
[ 8 2 2 14]
[ 4 6 7 15]
 [15 3 17 17]]
```

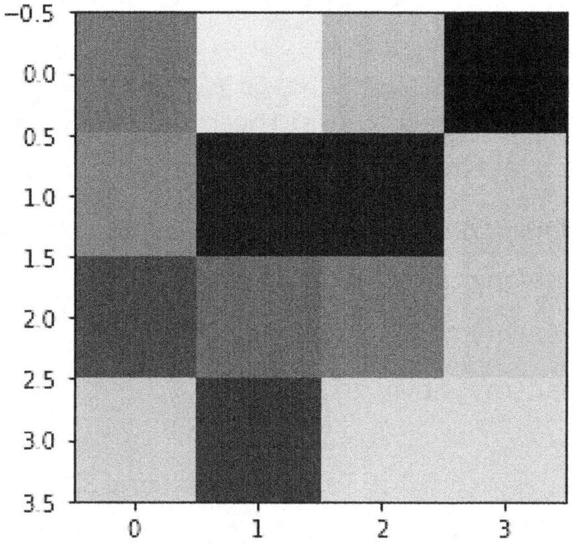

Further Readings – Basics of NumPy

1. Check the official documentation here (https://bit.ly/3oJRxE3) to learn more about NumPy.
2. You can learn more about Matplotlib at this link (https://matplotlib.org/)

Hands-on Time – Exercise

Now, it is your turn. Follow the instructions in **the exercises below** to check your understanding of Python tips and tricks that you learned in this chapter. The answers to these questions are given at the end of the book.

Exercise 4.1

Question 1:

Which function is used to find the mean across columns in a two-dimensional NumPy array?

A. np.mean(my_array, axis = 0)

B. np.mean(my_array, axis = 1)

C. np.mean(my_array, axis = 'col')

D. np.mean(my_array, axis = 'c')

Question 2:

Which function is used to find the frequency of each unique item in a NumPy array?

A. np.unique(my_array, return_counts=1)

B. np.unique(my_array, return_freq=1)

C. np.unique(my_array, return_counts=True)

D. np.unique(my_array, return_freq=True)

Question 3:

Which of the following functions can be used to load a CSV file into a NumPy array?

A. genfromtxt()

B. loadtxt()

C. loadcsv()

D. genfromcsv()

Exercise 4.2

Generate a NumPy array of shape 5 x 7, containing random integers between 1 and 50. Find the mean, median, and minimum and maximum values across columns and rows.

5

Arithmetic and Linear Algebra Operations with NumPy

5.1. Arithmetic Operations with NumPy

NumPy arrays provide a variety of functions to perform arithmetic operations. Some of these functions are explained in this section.

5.1.1. Finding Square Roots

The **sqrt()** function is used to find the square roots of all the elements in a list, as shown below:

Script 1:

```
importnumpyasnp

nums = [10,20,30,40,50]
np_sqr = np.sqrt(nums)
print(np_sqr)
```

Output:

```
[3.16227766 4.47213595 5.47722558 6.32455532 7.07106781]
```

5.1.2. Finding Logs

The **log()** function is used to find the logs of all the elements in a list, as shown below:

Script 2:

```
importnumpyasnp

nums = [10,20,30,40,50]
np_log = np.log(nums)
print(np_log )
```

Output:

```
[2.30258509 2.99573227 3.40119738 3.68887945 3.91202301]
```

5.1.3. Finding Exponents

The **exp()** function takes the exponents of all the elements in a list, as shown below:

Script 3:

```
importnumpyasnp

nums = [10,20,30,40,50]
np_exp = np.exp(nums)
print(np_exp)
```

Output:

```
[2.20264658e+04 4.85165195e+08 1.06864746e+13 2.35385267e+17
 5.18470553e+21]
```

5.1.4. Finding Sine and Cosine

You can find the sines and cosines of items in a list using the sine and cosine function, respectively, as shown in the following script.

Script 4:

```
importnumpyasnp

nums = [10,20,30,40,50]
np_sine = np.sin(nums)
print(np_sine)

nums = [10,20,30,40,50]
np_cos = np.cos(nums)
print(np_cos)
```

Output:

```
[-0.54402111 0.91294525 -0.98803162 0.74511316 -0.26237485]
[-0.83907153 0.40808206 0.15425145 -0.66693806 0.96496603]
```

5.2. NumPy for Linear Algebra Operations

Data science makes extensive use of linear algebra. The support for performing advanced linear algebra functions quickly and efficiently makes NumPy one of the most routinely used libraries for data science. In this section, you will perform some of the most linear algebraic operations with NumPy.

5.2.1. Finding the Matrix Dot Product

To find a matrix dot product, you can use the **dot()** function. To find the dot product, the number of columns in the first matrix must match the number of rows in the second matrix. Here is an example.

Script 5:

```
importnumpyasnp

A = np.random.randn(4,5)
B = np.random.randn(5,4)

Z = np.dot(A,B)
print(Z)
```

Output:

```
[[-0.4214615  0.16727233 0.81098999 -0.38015071]
 [-1.45721887 -0.42227335 -1.24713671 3.88470664]
 [-1.7216635  0.14865297 0.00539785 1.32007889]
[ 0.40891083 -0.53476366 1.00328983 -1.88270972]]
```

5.2.2. Element-wise Matrix Multiplication

In addition to finding the dot product of two matrices, you can element-wise multiply two matrices. To do so, you can use the **multiply()** function. However, the dimensions of the two matrices must match.

Script 6:

```
importnumpyasnp

row1 = [10,12,13]
row2 = [45,32,16]
row3 = [45,32,16]

nums_2d = np.array([row1, row2, row3])
multiply = np.multiply(nums_2d, nums_2d)
print(multiply)
```

Output:

```
[[ 100 144 169]
 [2025 1024 256]
 [2025 1024 256]]
```

5.2.3. Finding the Matrix Inverse

You find the inverse of a matrix via the **linalg.inv()** function, as shown below:

Script 7:

```
importnumpyasnp

row1 = [1,2,3]
row2 = [5,2,8]
row3 = [9,1,10]

nums_2d = np.array([row1, row2, row3])

inverse = np.linalg.inv(nums_2d)
print(inverse)
```

Output:

```
[[ 0.70588235 -1.      0.58823529]
[ 1.29411765 -1.      0.41176471]
 [-0.76470588 1.      -0.47058824]]
```

5.2.4. Finding the Matrix Determinant

Similarly, the determinant of a matrix can be found using the **linalg.det()** function, as shown below:

Script 8:

```
importnumpyasnp

row1 = [1,2,3]
row2 = [5,2,8]
row3 = [9,1,10]

nums_2d = np.array([row1, row2, row3])

determinant = np.linalg.det(nums_2d)
print(determinant)
```

Output:

```
17.0
```

5.2.5. Finding the Matrix Trace

The trace of a matrix refers to the sum of all the elements along the diagonal of a matrix. To find the trace of a matrix, you can use the **trace()** function, as shown below:

Script 9:

```
importnumpyasnp

row1 = [1,2,3]
row2 = [4,5,6]
row3 = [7,8,9]

nums_2d = np.array([row1, row2, row3])

trace = np.trace(nums_2d)
print(trace)
```

Output:

```
15
```

5.2.6. Solving a System of Linear Equations with Python

Now that you know how to use the NumPy library to perform various linear algebra functions, let's try to solve a system of linear equations, which is one of the most basic problems in linear algebra.

A system of linear equations refers to a collection of equations with some unknown variables. Solving a system of linear equations refers to finding the values of the unknown variables in equations. One of the ways to solve a system of linear equations is via matrices. Let's see how to do this.

Let's try to solve the following system of linear equations:

```
6x + 3y = 42
2x + 4y = 32
```

You have to convert the above equations into matrix and vector form. Let's name our matrix as A and the vector as B.

The number of rows in matrix A will be equal to the number of equations, and the number of columns will be equal to the number of variables. In our case, matrix A will consist of two rows and two columns. Therefore, the values in matrix A will be the constant terms on the left side of the equality symbol in the above equations, as shown below:

$$A = \begin{bmatrix} 6 & 3 \\ 2 & 4 \end{bmatrix}$$

The vector B will be a vector of size N, where N is the number of equations in the system of linear equations. The values in the vector B will be the values on the right side of the equals operator in the system of linear equations. The vector B will look like this:

$$B = \begin{bmatrix} 42 \\ 32 \end{bmatrix}$$

Finally, you need to create another vector that contains the values for your unknown variables. Let's name that Vector X, which looks like this:

$$X = \begin{bmatrix} x \\ y \end{bmatrix}$$

The system of linear equations can now be written as:

$$AX = B$$

And to find the value of the unknown variables, you can use the following equation:

$$X = (A^{-1}) \text{ dot } (B)$$

The above equation states that when you take the inverse of matrix A and then take its dot product with matrix B, the resultant matrix X will contain the values of the unknown variables.

Let's see how you can do this with the NumPy array.

The following script creates the NumPy arrays A and B for our matrices A and B, respectively.

Script 10:

```
importnumpyasnp

A = np.array([[6, 3],
[2, 4]])

B = np.array([42, 32])
```

Next, the script below finds the inverse of the matrix A using the inv() method from the linalg submodule from the NumPy module.

Script 11:

```
A_inv = np.linalg.inv(A)
print(A_inv)
```

Output:

```
[[ 0.22222222 -0.16666667]
 [-0.11111111 0.33333333]]
```

Finally, the script below takes the dot product of the inverse of matrix A with matrix B (which is a vector in our case).

Script 12:

```
X = np.dot(A_inv, B)
print(X)
```

Output:

```
[4. 6.]
```

The output shows that in our system of linear equations, the values of the unknown variables x and y are 4 and 6, respectively. You can put these values in the above equations and see if you get the correct answers.

Further Readings – Basics of NumPy

1. Check the official documentation here (https://bit.ly/3oJRxE3) to learn more about NumPy.
2. To learn more about the linalg submodule, check this link: https://bit.ly/3GsIIF1.

Hands-on Time – Exercises

Now, it is your turn. Follow the instructions in **the exercises below** to check your understanding of NumPy arithmetic and linear algebra functionalities. The answers to these questions are given at the end of the book.

Exercise 5.1

Question 1:

How do you find the dot product between two numpy arrays, A and B?

A. numpy.dot(A,B)

B. A.dot(B)

C. Both A and B

D. None of the above

Question 2:

How do you find the determinant of a matrix A?

A. numpy.linalg.det(A)

B. numpy.det(A)

C. linalg.det(A)

D. All of the above

Question 3:

How do you find the sine of an item in a NumPy array?

A. numpy.sine()

B. numpy.sin()

C. numpy.linalg.sin()

D. None of the above

Exercise 5.2

Solve the following system of three linear equations and find the values of the variables x, y, and z:

```
3x + 4y + 2z = 17

5x + 2y + 3z = 23

4x + 3y + 2z = 19
```

6

Implementing a Deep Neural Network with NumPy

In this chapter, you will briefly study the theory behind the different types of neural networks. You will study a simple densely connected neural network (DNN), a convolutional neural network (CNN), a recurrent neural network (RNN), and LSTM (which is a type of recurrent neural network).

In chapters 9, 10, and 11, you will see the practical implementation of deep neural networks for natural language processing.

6.1. Neural Network with a Single Output

In this section, you will implement a densely connected neural network with a single output from scratch. In addition, you will be learning how to find a non-linear boundary to separate two classes.

Let's start by defining our dataset first:

Script 1:

```
fromsklearnimport datasets
importnumpyasnp
importmatplotlib.pyplotasplt
%matplotlib inline

np.random.seed(0)
X, y = datasets.make_moons(100, noise=0.10)
x1 = X[:,0]
x2 = X[:,1]

plt.figure(figsize=(10,7))
plt.scatter(x1, x2, c= y, cmap=plt.cm.coolwarm)
```

Output:

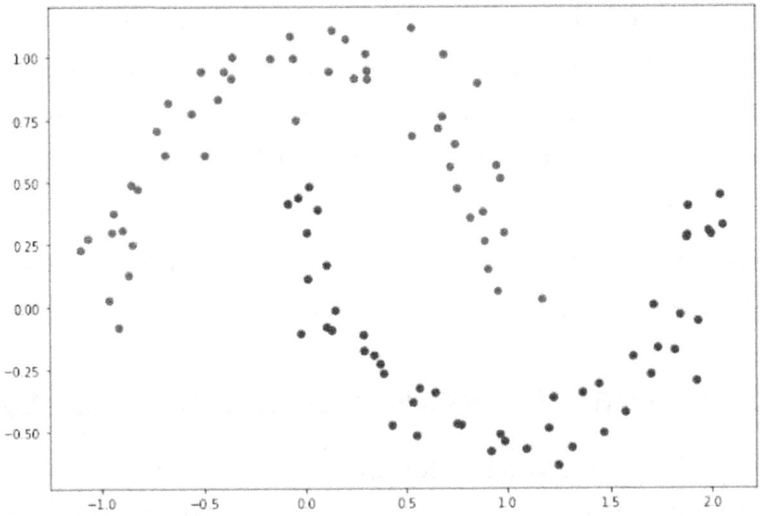

Our dataset has 100 records with two features and one output. You will need to reshape the output so that it has the same structure as the input features.

Script 2:

```
y = y.reshape(y.shape[0],1)
```

We can now check the shape of our input features and output labels.

Script 3:

```
print(X.shape)
print(y.shape)
```

Output:

```
(100, 2)
(100, 1)
```

Before we move forward, let's define the structure of our neural network. Our neural network will look like this:

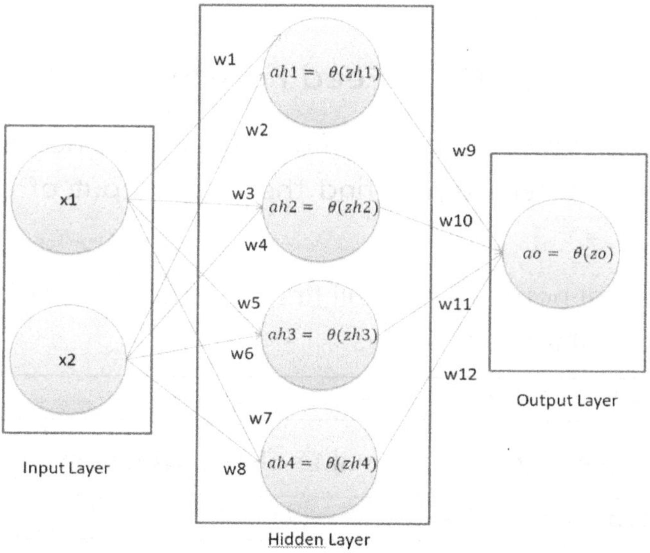

In a neural network, we have an input layer, one or multiple hidden layers, and an output layer. In our neural network, we have two nodes in the input layer (since there are two features in the input), one hidden layer with four nodes, and one output layer with one node since we are doing binary classification. The number of hidden layers and the number of neurons per hidden layer depend upon you.

In the above neural network, x1 and x2 are the input features, and ao is the output of the network. Here, the only thing we can control is the weights w1, w2, w3, ... w12. The idea is to find the values of weights for which the difference between the predicted output, ao in this case, and the actual output (labels) is minimum.

A neural network works in two steps:

1. Feed Forward
2. BackPropagation

I will explain both these steps in the context of our neural network.

6.1.1. Feed Forward

In the feed forward step, the final output of a neural network is created. So let's try to find the final output of our neural network.

In our neural network, we will first find the value of zh1, which can be calculated as follows:

```
zh1 = x1w1 + x2w2 + b ---------- (1)
```

Using zh1, we can find the value of ah1, which is:

```
ah1 = sigmoid(zh1)  ---------- (2)
```

In the same way, you find the values of ah2, ah3, and ah4.

To find the value of zo, you can use the following formula:

```
zo = ah1w9 + ah2w10 + ah3w11 + ah4w12  --------- (3)
```

Finally, to find the output of the neural network ao, use the following formula:

```
ao = sigmoid(zo) ---------- (4)
```

6.1.2. Backpropagation

The purpose of backpropagation is to minimize the overall loss by finding the optimum values of weights. The loss function we are going to use in this section is the mean squared error, which is, in our case, represented as:

$$J = \frac{1}{m} \sum_{i=1}^{m} (ao_i - y_i)^2$$

Here, ao is the predicted output from our neural network, and y is the actual output.

Our weights are divided into two parts. We have weights that connect input features to the hidden layer and the hidden layer to the output node. We call the weights that connect the input to the hidden layer collectively as wh (w1, w2, w3 ... w8), and the weights connecting the hidden layer to the output as wo (w9, w10, w11, w12).

The backpropagation will consist of two phases. In the first phase, we will find dcost_dwo (which refers to the derivative of the total cost with respect to wo (weights in the output layer)). By the chain rule, dcost_dwo can be represented as the product of dcost_dao * dao_dzo * dzo_dwo. (d here refers to derivative.) Mathematically:

```
dcost_dwo = dcost_dao * dao_dzo * dzo_dwo ------ (5)
dcost_dao = 1/m (ao - y)  ------- (6)
dao_dzo = sigmoid(zo) * ( 1 - sigmoid(zo)) ------- (7)
dzo_dwo = ah.T ------ 8
```

In the same way, you find the derivative of cost with respect to bias in the output layer, i.e., dcost_dbo, which is given as:

```
dcost_dbo = dcost_dao * dao_dzo
```

Putting 6, 7, and 8 in equation 5, we can get the derivative of cost with respect to the output weights.

The next step is to find the derivative of cost with respect to hidden layer weights, wh, and bias bh. Let's first find the derivative of cost with respect to hidden layer weights:

```
dcost_dwh =dcost_dah * dah_dzh * dzh_dwh ….. (9)

dcost_dah= dcost_dao * dao_dzo * dzo_dah ……. (10)
```

The values of dcost_dao and dao_dzo can be calculated from equations 6 and 7, respectively. The value of dzo_dah is given as:

```
dzo_dah = wo.T …… (11)
```

Putting the values of equations 6, 7, and 11 in equation 11, you can get the value of equation 10.

Next, let's find the value of dah_dzh:

```
dah_dzh = sigmoid(zh)*(1-sigmoid(zh) ….. (12)
and,
dzh_dwh = X.T (13)
```

Using equations 10, 12, and 13 in equation 9, you can find the value of dcost_dwh.

Finally, you can update the weights of the output and hidden layers as:

```
wo = wo - (lr *dcost_dwo)
wh = wh- (lr * dcost_dwh)
```

In the above equations, *wo* refers to all the weights in the output layer, whereas *wh* refers to the weights in the hidden layers.

6.1.3. Implementation with NumPy Library

In this section, you will implement the neural network that we saw earlier from scratch in Python. Let's define a function that defines the parameters:

Script 4:

```
defdefine_parameters(weights):
weight_list = []
bias_list = []
foriinrange(len(weights) - 1):

    w = np.random.randn(weights[i], weights[i+1])
    b = np.random.randn()

weight_list.append(w)
bias_list.append(b)

returnweight_list, bias_list
```

Now, since we have multiple sets of weights, the defined parameters function will return the list of weights connecting the input and hidden layer and the hidden and output layer.

Next, we define the sigmoid function and its derivative:

Script 5:

```
defsigmoid(x):
return1/(1+np.exp(-x))
```

Script 6:

```
defsigmoid_der(x):
return sigmoid(x)*(1-sigmoid(x))
```

The feed forward part of the algorithm is implemented by the **`prediction()`** method, as shown below:

Script 7:

```
defpredictions(w, b, X):
zh = np.dot(X,w[0]) + b[0]
  ah = sigmoid(zh)

  zo = np.dot(ah, w[1]) + b[1]
ao = sigmoid(zo)
returnao
```

The following script defines the cost function:

Script 8:

```
deffind_cost(ao,y):
  m = y.shape[0]
total_cost = (1/m) * np.sum(np.square(ao - y))
returntotal_cost
```

Finally, to implement the backpropagation, we define a **find_derivatives()** function, as follows:

Script 9:

```
deffind_derivatives(w, b, X):

zh = np.dot(X,w[0]) + b[0]
  ah = sigmoid(zh)

  zo = np.dot(ah, w[1]) + b[1]
ao = sigmoid(zo)

# Backpropagation phase 1
m = y.shape[0]
dcost_dao = (1/m)*(ao-y)
dao_dzo = sigmoid_der(zo)
dzo_dwo = ah.T

dwo= np.dot(dzo_dwo, dcost_dao * dao_dzo)
dbo = np.sum(dcost_dao * dao_dzo)
```

```
# Backpropagation phase 2

# dcost_wh = dcost_dah * dah_dzh * dzh_dwh
# dcost_dah = dcost_dzo * dzo_dah

dcost_dzo = dcost_dao * dao_dzo
dzo_dah = w[1].T

dcost_dah = np.dot(dcost_dzo , dzo_dah)

dah_dzh = sigmoid_der(zh)
dzh_dwh = X.T
dwh = np.dot(dzh_dwh, dah_dzh * dcost_dah)
dbh = np.sum(dah_dzh * dcost_dah)

returndwh, dbh, dwo, dbo
```

And to update weights by subtracting the gradient, we define the **update_weights()** function.

Script 10:

```
defupdate_weights(w,b,dwh, dbh, dwo, dbo, lr):
w[0] = w[0] - lr * dwh
w[1] = w[1] - lr * dwo

b[0] = b[0] - lr * dbh
b[1] = b[1] - lr * dbo

return w, b
```

Here is the **my_neural_network** class, which is used to train the neural network by implementing the feed forward and backward propagation steps.

Script 11:

```
defmy_neural_network(X, y, lr, epochs):
error_list = []
input_len = X.shape[1]
output_len = y.shape[1]
w,b = define_parameters([input_len, 4, output_len])

foriinrange(epochs):
ao = predictions(w, b, X)
    cost = find_cost(ao, y)
error_list.append(cost)
dwh, dbh, dwo, dbo = find_derivatives (w, b, X)
    w, b = update_weights(w, b, dwh, dbh, dwo, dbo, lr )
ifi % 50 == 0 :
print(cost)

return w, b, error_list
```

Let's train our neural network now to see the error reducing:

Script 12:

```
lr = 0.5
epochs = 2000
w, b, error_list = my_neural_network(X,y,lr,epochs)
```

Output:

```
0.1980211046202944
0.14097327813016874
0.1199356196746553
0.10996149384567079
0.1046354602995857
0.10125014770369335
0.09877988582294377
0.09681954900387213
0.09519153134310644
0.09380667924462933
0.09261322597192048
0.09157694024355723
0.09067287831113126
0.0898816633148205
0.08918762513676567
0.08857775866745798
```

```
0.0880410781190082
0.08756818639880107
0.08715097414153263
0.08678240229725143
0.08645634002244419
0.08616743928189777
0.08591103380363199
0.08568305442008338
0.0854799559120146
0.08529865252129894
0.08513646055443663
0.08499104719247362
0.08486038495701591
0.08474271141085092
0.08463649370001301
0.08454039753494193
0.08445326019470517
0.08437406713419247
0.08430193178325884
0.08423607814745766
0.0841758258488823
0.08412057727921075
0.08406980657236514
0.08402305013908634
```

In the output, you can see that the error is reducing. Let's plot the error value on a plot:

Script 13:

```
plt.plot(error_list)
```

Output:

```
[<matplotlib.lines.Line2D at 0x7f8e094b94e0>]
```

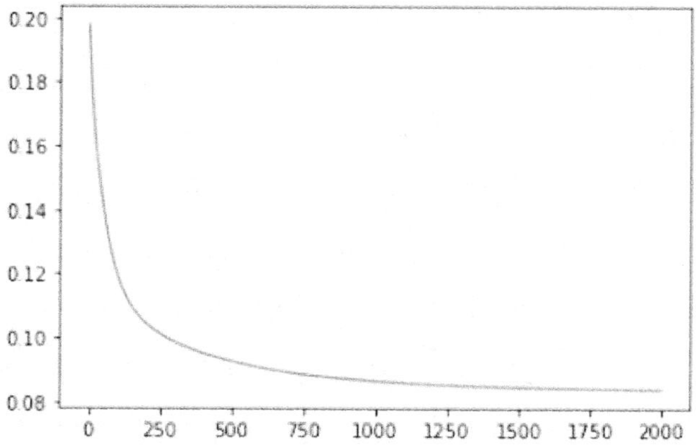

You can see that the error is decreasing with each epoch.

The process of implementing a neural network with one output from scratch in Python is very similar to logistic regression. However, in this case, we had to update two sets of weights, one in the hidden layer and one in the output layer.

6.2. Neural Network with Multiple Outputs

In the previous section, you did a binary classification where you predicted whether a point is red or blue. However, in most real-world applications, you have to classify between more than two objects. For instance, you might be given an image, and you have to guess the single digit in the image. In that case, the number of possible outputs will be 0–9 = 10. The types of problems where you have more than two possible outputs are called multiclass classification problems.

To implement multiclass classification problems, you have to make three changes in the neural network with a single output. The changes are as follows:

1. The number of nodes in the output layer should be equal to the number of possible outputs.
2. The Softmax activation function should be used in the final output layer.
3. To reduce the cost, a negative log-likelihood function should be used as the loss function.

We will not go into the details of the Softmax and negative log-likelihood functions in this chapter. Here is a very good blog to understand the Softmax function: https://bit.ly/3dXPWSY

And here is a very good blog to understand the negative log likelihood: https://bit.ly/2BYlOc7

In this section, we will develop a neural network with three possible outputs. Let's first create the dataset for that.

Execute the following script:

Script 14:

```
importnumpyasnp
importmatplotlib.pyplotasplt

np.random.seed(42)

cat1 = np.random.randn(800, 2) + np.array([0, -3])
cat2 = np.random.randn(800, 2) + np.array([3, 3])
cat3 = np.random.randn(800, 2) + np.array([-3, 3])

X = np.vstack([cat1, cat2, cat3])

labels = np.array([0]*800 + [1]*800 + [2]*800)

y = np.zeros((2400, 3))

foriinrange(2400):
y[i, labels[i]] = 1
```

Let's check the shape of our dataset.

Script 15:

```
print(X.shape)
print(y.shape)
```

Output:

```
(2400, 2)
(2400, 3)
```

The output shows that we have 2,400 records in our dataset. The input contains two features, and the output contains three possible labels. (Each row in the output contains three columns, one column for each label.)

Next, we will plot our dataset to see the three classes:

Script 16:

```
x1 = X[:,0]
x2 = X[:,1]

plt.figure(figsize=(10,7))
plt.scatter(x1, x2, c= y, cmap=plt.cm.coolwarm)
```

Output:

```
<matplotlib.collections.PathCollection at 0x7f289391fe48>
```

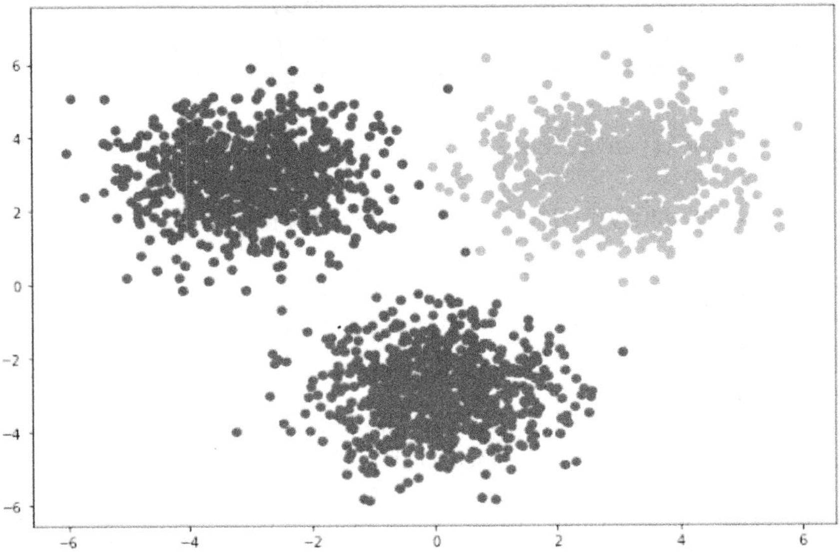

From the output, you can see that our dataset records can either be represented by a red, green, or blue dot, which means that we have three possible labels in the output. Also, these labels cannot be separated by a straight line. Hence, we will be using a neural network with multiple outputs. The architecture of the neural network will look like this:

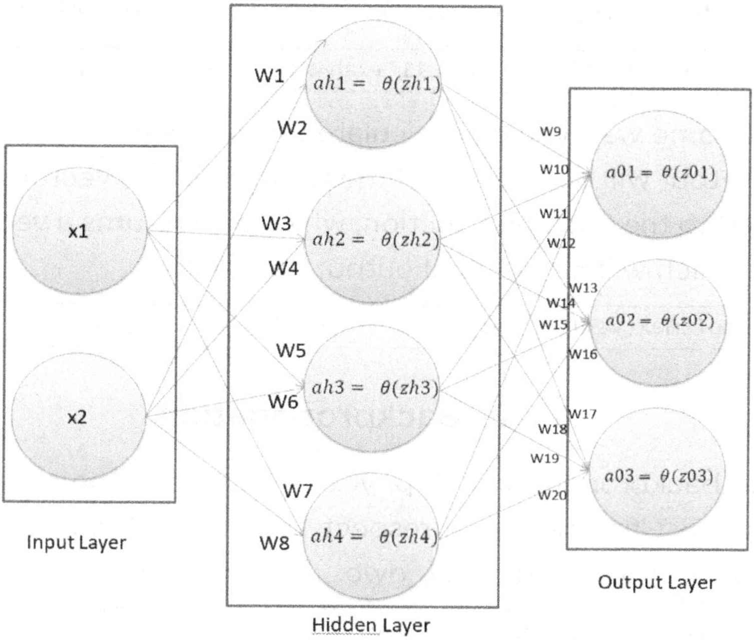

You can see that this neural network is very similar to the neural network that we saw earlier. Except, now we have three nodes in the output, and hence, a greater number of weights in the output layer. Let's see the feed forward process for the above neural network:

6.2.1. Feed Forward

Let's briefly review the feed forward step for a neural network with multiple steps. To calculate the value of zh1, the following equation is used:

```
zh1 = x1w1 + x2w2 + b ---------- (14)
```

Using zh1, we can find the value of ah1, which is:

```
ah1 = sigmoid(zh1)  ---------- (15)
```

In the same way, you find the values of ah2, ah3, and ah4.

To find the value of zo, you can use the following formula:

```
zo1 = ah1w9 + ah2w10 + ah3w11 + ah4w12  --------- (16)
```

In the same way, you can calculate the values for zo2 and zo3. The output will be a vector of the form [3,1]. This vector will be passed to the Softmax function, which also returns a vector of [3,1], which will be our final output ao. Hence,

```
ao = softmax(vector [zo]) ---------- (17)
```

6.2.2. Backpropagation

In the backpropagation step, you have to find the derivative of the cost function with respect to the weights in different layers. Let's first find dcost_dwo:

```
dcost_dwo = dcost_dzo * dzo_dwo ------ (18)
```

The derivative of a negative log-likelihood function with respect to the values in the zo vector is:

```
dcost_dzo = ao - y -------- (19)
```

In equation 19, y is the actual output. Similarly, we can find dzo_dwo, as follows:

```
dzo_dwo = ah.T ----- (20)
```

Putting equations 19 and 20 in equations 18, you can get the derivate of cost with respect to the weights in the output layer, i.e., wo.

Similarly, dcost_dbo is equal to:

```
dcost_dbo = dcost_dzo ---- (21)
```

Next, we need to find the dcost_dwh, which is given as:

```
dcost_dwh = dcost_dah* dah_dzh * dzh_dwh ------ (22)

dcost_dah = dcost_dzo * dzo_dah ---- (23)

dzo_dah = wo.T -------- (24)
```

Putting the value of equations 19 and 24 in equation 23, you can get the value of dcost_dah.

Next,

```
dah_dzh = sigmoid(zh) * (1- sigmoid(zh) ------- (25)

dzh_dwh = ah.T ------------ (26)
```

Putting the value of equations 23, 25, and 26 in equation 22, you can find the value of dost_dwh.

Finally, as previously, you can update the weights of the output and hidden layers as:

```
wo = wo - (lr *dcost_dwo)

wh = wh- (lr * dcost_dwh)
```

In the above equations, *wo* refers to all the weights in the output layer, whereas *wh* refers to the weights in the hidden layers.

6.2.3. Implementation with NumPy Library

Let's now see the Python implementation of a neural network with multiple outputs:

Script 17:

```
importnumpyasnp
importmatplotlib.pyplotasplt

np.random.seed(42)

cat1 = np.random.randn(800, 2) + np.array([0, -3])
cat2 = np.random.randn(800, 2) + np.array([3, 3])
cat3 = np.random.randn(800, 2) + np.array([-3, 3])


X = np.vstack([cat1, cat2, cat3])

labels = np.array([0]*800 + [1]*800 + [2]*800)

y = np.zeros((2400, 3))

foriinrange(2400):
y[i, labels[i]] = 1


defdefine_parameters(weights):
weight_list = []
bias_list = []
foriinrange(len(weights) - 1):

    w = np.random.randn(weights[i], weights[i+1])
    b = np.random.randn()

weight_list.append(w)
bias_list.append(b)

returnweight_list, bias_list

defsoftmax(X):
expX = np.exp(X)
returnexpX / expX.sum(axis=1, keepdims=True)

defsigmoid(x):
return1/(1+np.exp(-x))
```

```
defsigmoid_der(x):
return sigmoid(x)*(1-sigmoid(x))


defpredictions(w, b, X):
zh = np.dot(X,w[0]) + b[0]
  ah = sigmoid(zh)

  zo = np.dot(ah, w[1]) + b[1]
ao = softmax(zo)
returnao


deffind_cost(ao,y):

total_cost = np.sum(-y * np.log(ao))
returntotal_cost

deffind_derivatives(w, b, X):

zh = np.dot(X,w[0]) + b[0]
  ah = sigmoid(zh)

  zo = np.dot(ah, w[1]) + b[1]
ao = softmax(zo)

# Backpropagation phase 1


dcost_dzo = (ao-y)
dzo_dwo = ah.T

dwo= np.dot(dzo_dwo, dcost_dzo)
dbo = np.sum(dcost_dzo)

# Backpropagation phase 2

# dcost_wh = dcost_dah * dah_dzh * dzh_dwh
# dcost_dah = dcost_dzo * dzo_dah
```

```
dzo_dah = w[1].T

dcost_dah = np.dot(dcost_dzo , dzo_dah)

dah_dzh = sigmoid_der(zh)
dzh_dwh = X.T
dwh = np.dot(dzh_dwh, dah_dzh * dcost_dah)
dbh = np.sum(dah_dzh * dcost_dah)

returndwh, dbh, dwo, dbo

defupdate_weights(w,b,dwh, dbh, dwo, dbo, lr):
w[0] = w[0] - lr * dwh
w[1] = w[1] - lr * dwo

b[0] = b[0] - lr * dbh
b[1] = b[1] - lr * dbo

return w, b

defmy_multiout_neural_network(X, y, lr, epochs):
error_list = []
input_len = X.shape[1]
output_len = y.shape[1]
w,b = define_parameters([input_len, 4, output_len])

foriinrange(epochs):
ao = predictions(w, b, X)
    cost = find_cost(ao, y)
error_list.append(cost)
dwh, dbh, dwo, dbo = find_derivatives (w, b, X)
    w, b = update_weights(w, b, dwh, dbh, dwo, dbo, lr )
ifi % 50 == 0 :
print(cost)

return w, b, error_list


lr = 0.0005
epochs = 1000
w, b, error_list = my_multiout_neural_network(X,y,lr,epochs)
```

Output:

```
4921.784443712775
115.05275654791413
60.7093977747567
43.422649664931626
34.88864651152795
29.785198170132094
26.38081266811703
23.942717399078127
22.107134982438154
20.67281284937415
19.519299319106253
18.570055076513714
17.774096074967886
17.09614091195548
16.51099321192574
16.000176100360964
15.549830828069574
15.149357906344129
14.790511529599819
14.466780088357714
```

The output shows that the error is decreasing. You might get slightly different error values since weights are randomly initialized. Let's plot the error against the epochs:

Script 18:

```
plt.plot(error_list)
```

Output:

```
[<matplotlib.lines.Line2D at 0x7f2893892908>]
```

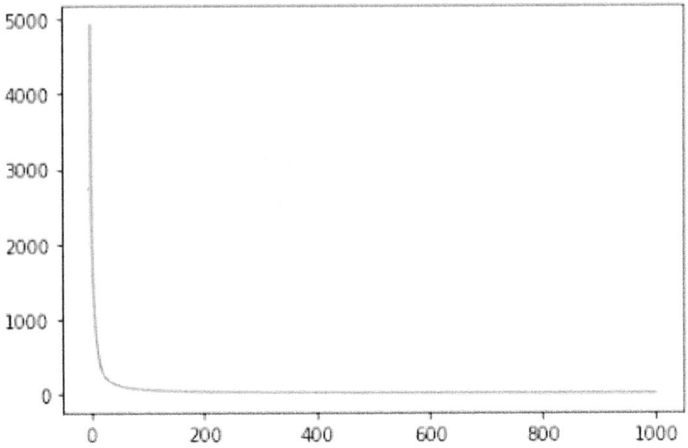

You can see the error decreasing quickly initially and then very slowly.

In this chapter, you saw how the NumPy library can be used to implement an artificial neural network from scratch, which is the foundation of various advanced artificial intelligence applications. From the next chapter, you will be introduced to Pandas, which is an extremely useful library for data manipulation, visualization, and analysis.

Further Readings - Basics of NumPy
1. Check the official documentation here (https://bit.ly/3oJRxE3) to learn more about NumPy. 2. You can learn more about neural networks and deep learning at this link (https://bit.ly/2SMpztU).

Hands-on Time - Exercises
Now, it is your turn. Follow the instructions in **the exercises below** to check your understanding of implementing Neural Networks with NumPy. The answers to these questions are given at the end of the book.

Exercise 6.1

Question 1:

In a neural network with three input features, one hidden layer of five nodes, and an output layer with three possible values, what will be the dimensions of weights that connect the input to the hidden layer? Remember, the dimensions of the input data are (m,3), where m is the number of records.

A. [5,3]

B. [3,5]

C. [4,5]

D. [5,4]

Question 2:

Which activation function do you use in the output layer in case of multiclass classification problems?

A. Sigmoid

B. Negative log likelihood

C. Relu

D. Softmax

Question 3:

Neural networks with hidden layers are capable of finding:

A. Linear Boundaries

B. Non-linear Boundaries

C. All of the above

D. None of the Above

Exercise 6.2

Try to classify the following dataset with three classes by implementing a multiclass classification neural network from scratch using the NumPy library in Python:

```
importnumpyasnp
importmatplotlib.pyplotasplt

np.random.seed(42)

cat1 = np.random.randn(800, 2) + np.array([0, -2])
cat2 = np.random.randn(800, 2) + np.array([2, 2])
cat3 = np.random.randn(800, 2) + np.array([-3, -3])

X = np.vstack([cat1, cat2, cat3])

labels = np.array([0]*800 + [1]*800 + [2]*800)

y = np.zeros((2400, 3))

foriinrange(2400):
y[i, labels[i]] = 1

x1 = X[:,0]
x2 = X[:,1]

plt.figure(figsize=(10,7))
plt.scatter(x1, x2, c= y, cmap=plt.cm.coolwarm)
```

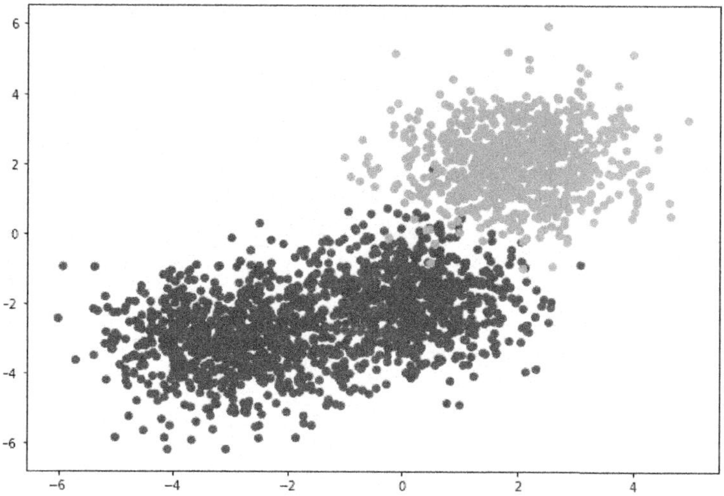
6
4
2
0
-2
-4
-6
-6
-4
-2
0
2
4

Appendix:

Working with Jupyter Notebook

All the scripts in this book are executed via Jupyter Notebook that comes with Anaconda or via the Colab Environment, which contains a Jupyter Notebook-like interface of its own. Therefore, it makes sense to give a brief overview of Jupyter Notebook.

In chapter 1, you have already seen how to run a very basic script with the Jupyter Notebook from Anaconda. In this section, you will see some other common functionalities of the Jupyter Notebook.

Creating a New Notebook

There are two main ways to create a new Python Jupyter notebook.

1. From the home page of the Jupyter notebook, click the **New** button at the top right corner and then select *Python 3*, as shown in the following screenshot.

2. If you have already opened a Jupyter notebook, and you want to create a new Jupyter notebook, select "File - > New Notebook" from the top menu. Here is a screenshot of how to do this.

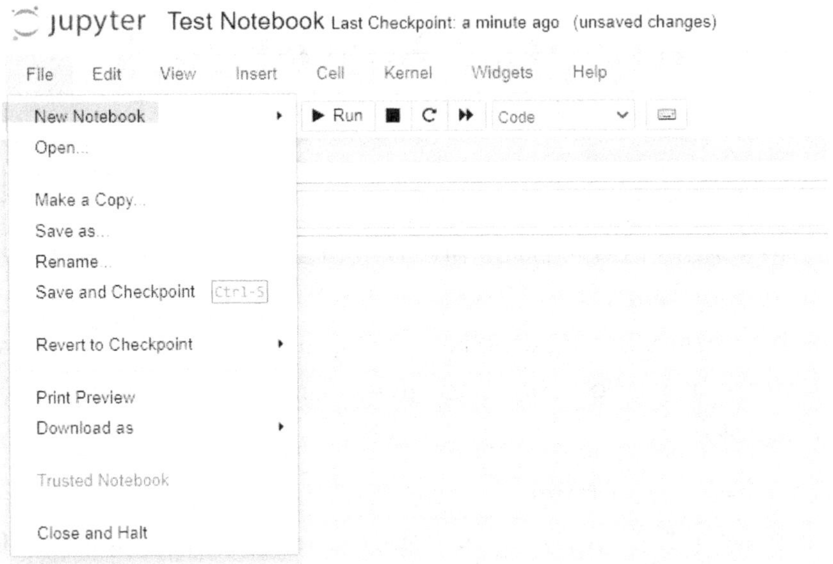

Renaming a Notebook

To rename a new Jupyter notebook, click on the Jupyter notebook name from the top left corner of your notebook. A dialog box will appear containing the old name of your Jupyter notebook, as shown below (the default name for a Jupyter notebook will be "Untitled"). Here, you can enter a new name for your Jupyter notebook.

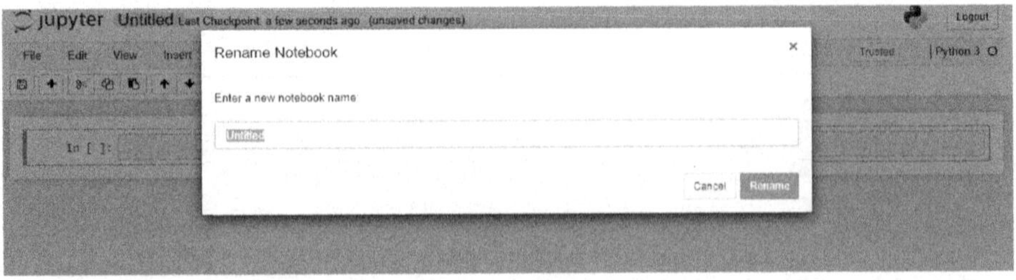

Running Script in a Cell

To run a script inside a cell, select the cell and then press "CTRL + Enter" from your keyboard. Your script will execute. However, a new cell will not be created automatically once the current cell executes.

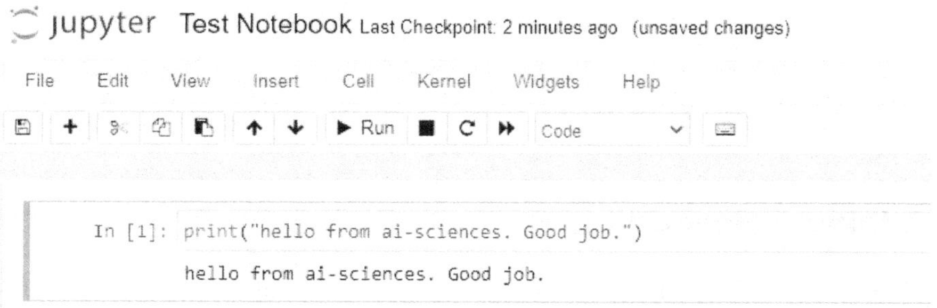

If you want to automatically create a new cell with the execution of a cell, you can select a cell and execute it using "SHIFT + ENTER" or "ALT + ENTER". You will see that the current cell is executed, and a new cell is automatically created, as shown below:

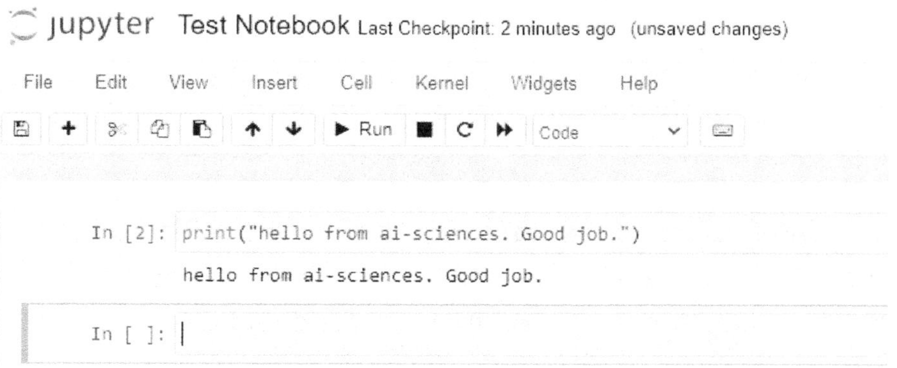

You can also run a cell by selecting a cell and then by clicking the **Run** option from the top menu, as shown below.

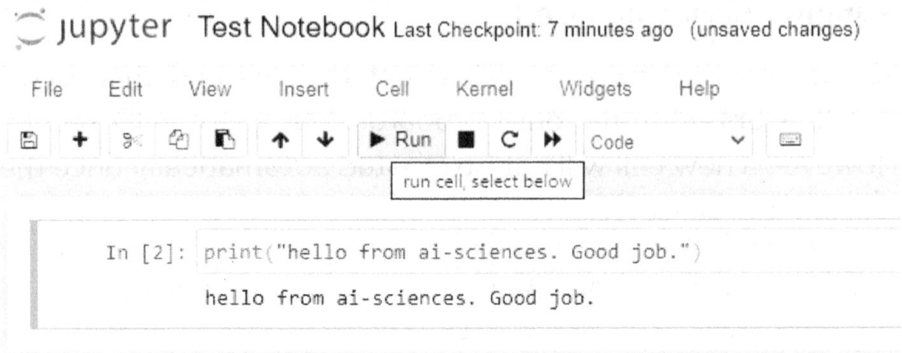

Adding a New Cell

The plus "+" symbol from the top menu allows you to add a new cell below the currently selected cell. Here is an example.

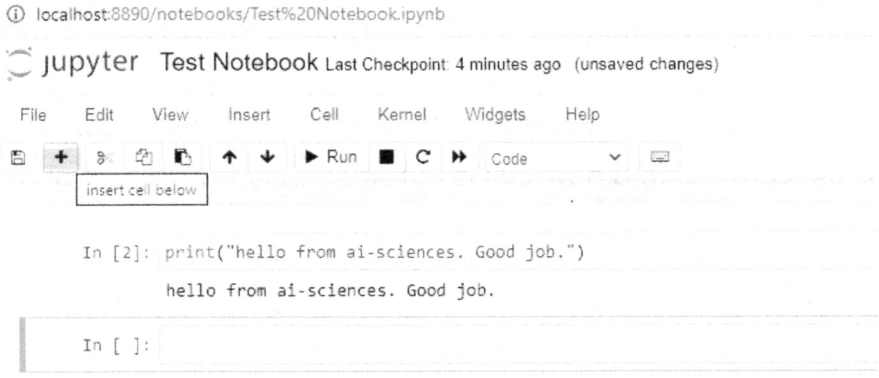

You can also insert cells above or below any selected cells via the *Insert Cell Above* and *Insert Cell Below* commands from the *Insert* option in the top menu, as shown below:

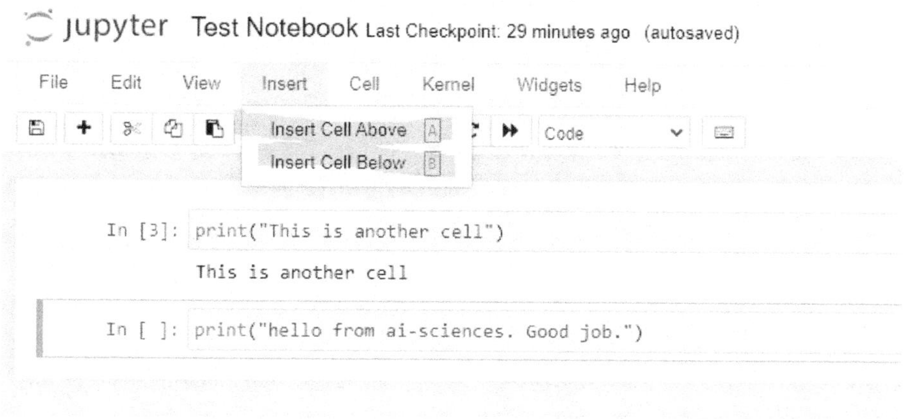

Deleting a New Cell

To delete a cell, simply select the cell and then click the scissor icon from the top menu of your Jupyter notebook, as shown in the following screenshot.

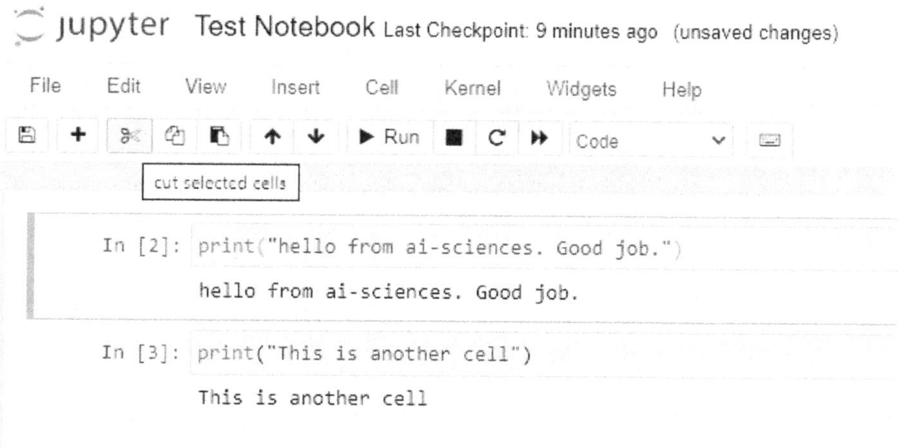

Moving Cells Up and Down

To move a cell down, select a cell and then click the downward arrow. Here is an example. Here, cell number 2 is moved one position below.

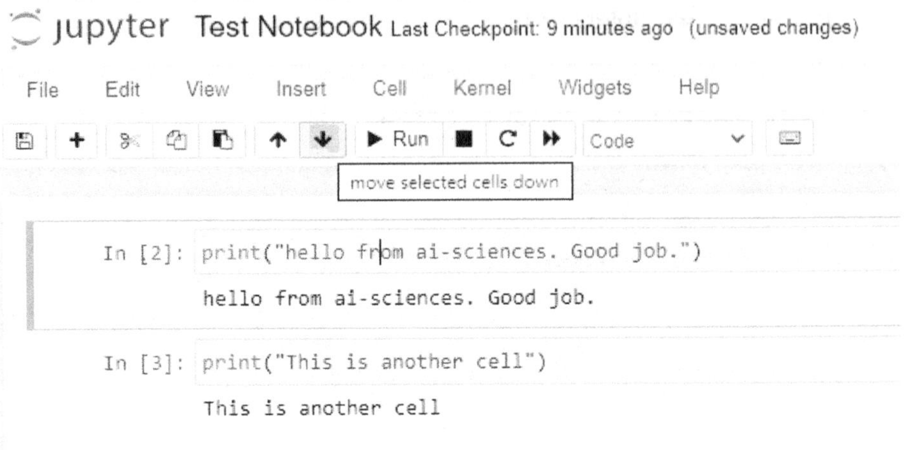

In the output, you can see that cell 2 is now below cell 3.

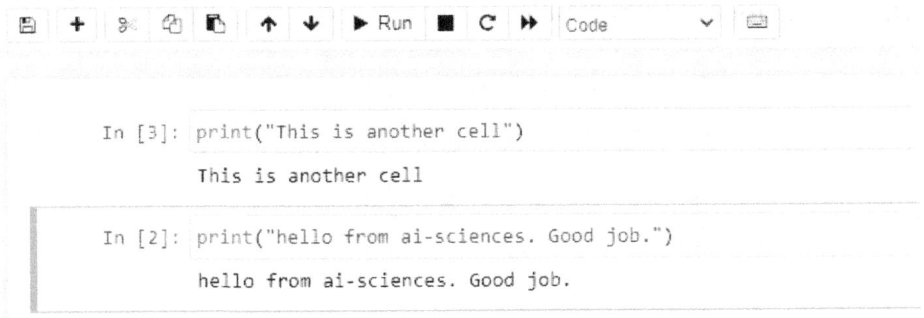

In the same way, you can click on the upward arrow to move a cell up.

Miscellaneous Kernel Options

To see miscellaneous kernel options, click the *Kernel* button from the top menu. A dropdown list will appear, where you can see options related to interrupting, restarting, reconnecting, and shutting down the kernel used to run your script. Clicking "Restart & Run" will restart the kernel and run all the cells once again.

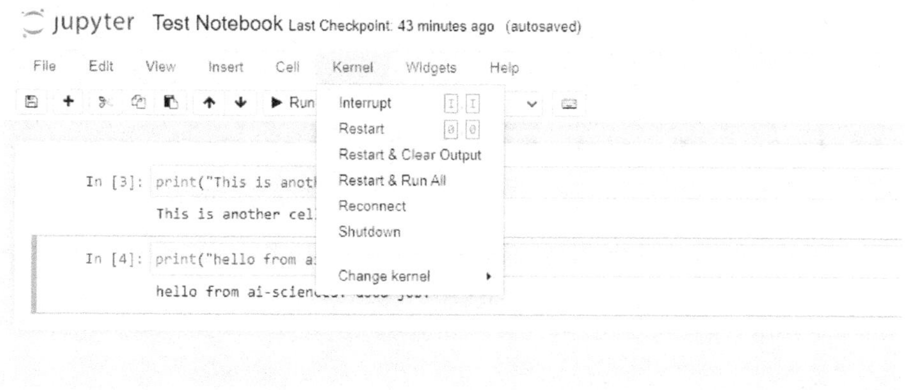

Miscellaneous Cell Options

Clicking the Cell button from the top menu reveals the location of options related to running a particular cell in a Jupyter notebook. Look at the following screenshot for reference.

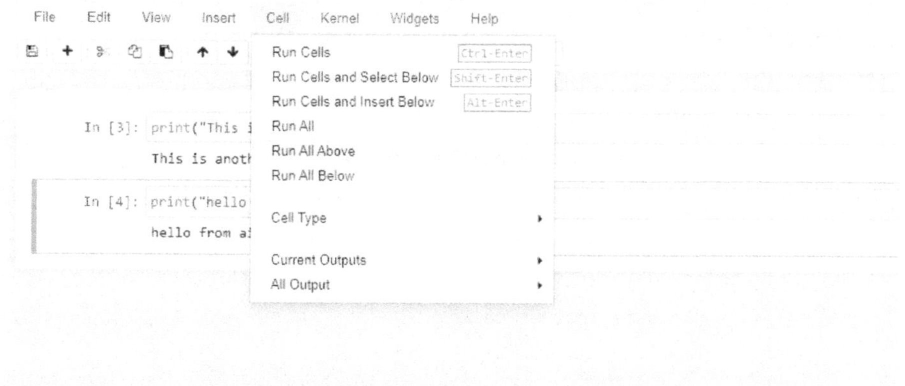

Writing Markdown in Jupyter Notebook

Apart from writing Python scripts, you can also write markdown content in the Jupyter notebook. To do so, you have to first select a cell where you want to add your markdown content, and then you have to select the *Markdown* option from the dropdown list, as shown in the following script.

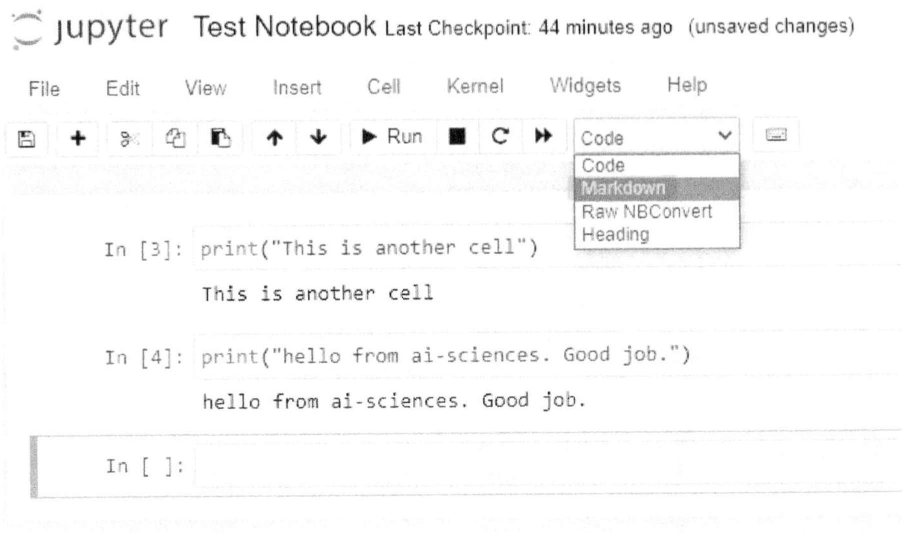

Next, you need to enter the markdown content in the markdown cell. For instance, in the following screenshot, the markdown content h2 level heading is added to the third cell.

When you run the 3rd cell in the above script, you will see the compiled markdown content, as shown below:

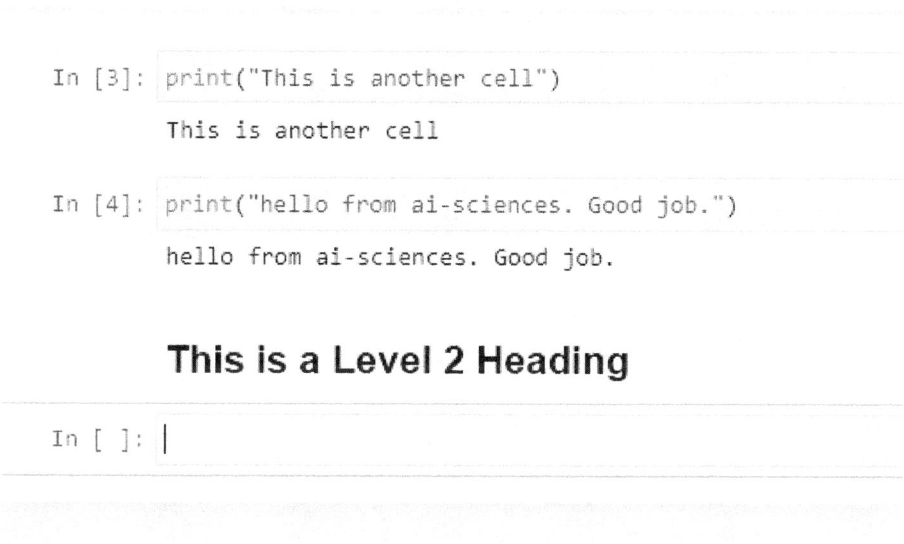

Downloading Jupyter Notebooks

To download a Jupyter notebook, click the "File -> Download as" option from the top menu. You can download Jupyter notebooks in various formats, e.g., HTML, PDF, Python Notebook (ipynb), etc.

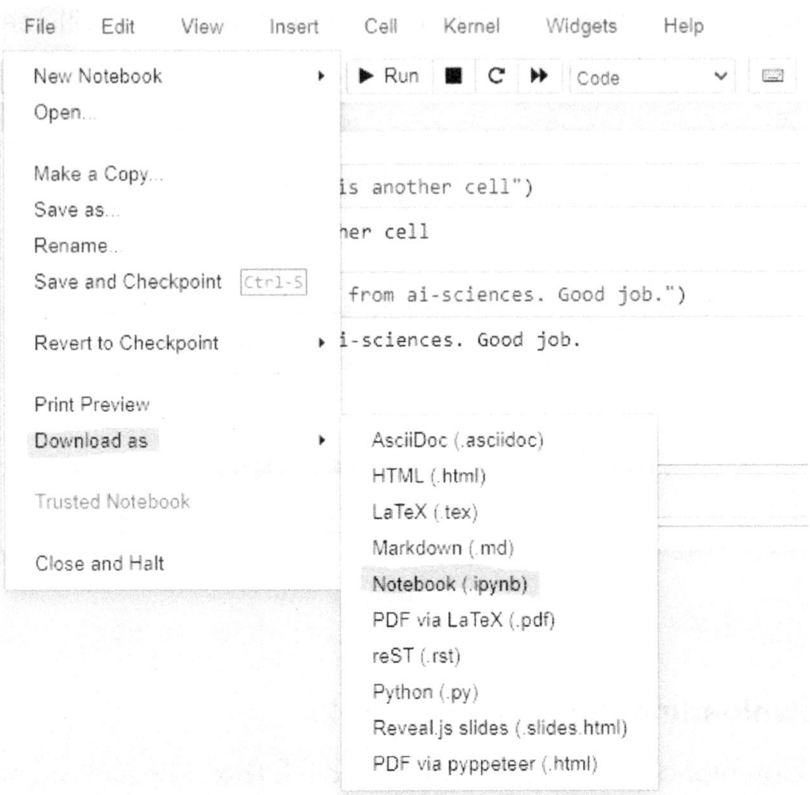

Uploading an Existing Notebook

Similarly, you can upload an existing notebook to Anaconda Jupyter. To do so, you need to click the *Upload* button from the main Jupyter dashboard. Look at the screenshot below for reference.

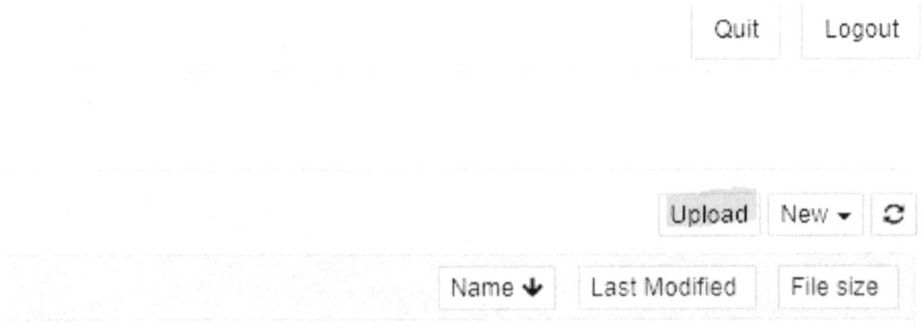

Exercise Solutions

Exercise 1.1

Question 1

Which iteration should be used when you want to repeatedly execute a code a specific number of times?

A. For Loop

B. While Loop

C. Both A & B

D. None of the above

Answer: A

Question 2

What is the maximum number of values that a function can return in Python?

A. Single Value

B. Double Value

C. More than two values

D. None

Answer: C

Question 3

Which of the following membership operators are supported by Python?

A. In

B. Out

C. Not In

D. Both A and C

Answer: D

Exercise 1.2

Print the table of integer 9 using a while loop:

```
j=1
   while j< 11:
     print("9 x "+str(j)+ " = "+ str(9*j))
     j=j+1
```

Exercise 2.1

Question 1:

To generate an identity matrix of 4 rows and 4 columns, which of the following functions can be used?

A. np.identity(4,4)

B. np.id(4,4)

C. np.eye(4,4)

D. All of the above

Answer: C

Question 2:

To delete a column from a two-dimensional NumPy array, the value of the axis attribute of the delete method should be set to:

A. 0

B. 1

C. column_number

D. All of the above

Answer: B

Question 3:

How to create the array of numbers 4,7,10,13,16 with NumPy?

A. np.arange(3, 16, 3)

B. np.arange(4, 16, 3)

C. np.arange(4, 15,3)

D. None of the above

Answer: D

Exercise 2.2

Create a random NumPy array of 5 rows and 4 columns.

Solution:

```
importnumpyasnp
uniform_random = np.random.rand(4, 5)
print(uniform_random)
```

Exercise 3.1

Question 1:

Which function is used to convert a multi-dimensional NumPy array into a flat array of 1-dimension?

A. np.reshape(0)

B. np.reshape(-1)

C. np.reshape(1)

D. None of the Above

Answer: B

Question 2:

Which function is used to save a NumPy array in text format?

A. np.savetext()

B. np.saveText()

C. np.saveTxt()

D. np.savetxt()

Answer: D

Question 3:

To sort a NumPy array in descending order, you can use the following function:

A. np.flipud(np.sort(my_array))

B. np.sort(np.flip(my_array))

C. np.sort()

D. np.flip()

Answer: A

Exercise 3.2

Create a random NumPy array of 4 rows and 5 columns. Then, using array indexing and slicing, display the items from row 3 to end and column 2 to end.

Solution:

```
uniform_random = np.random.rand(4, 5)
print(uniform_random)
print("Result")
print(uniform_random[2:,1:])
```

Exercise 4.1

Question 1:

Which function is used to find the mean across columns in a two-dimensional NumPy array?

A. np.mean(my_array, axis = 0)

B. np.mean(my_array, axis = 1)

C. np.mean(my_array, axis = 'col')

D. np.mean(my_array, axis = 'c')

Answer: B

Question 2:

Which function is used to find the frequency of each unique item in a NumPy array?

A. np.unique(my_array, return_counts=1)

B. np.unique(my_array, return_freq=1)

C. np.unique(my_array, return_counts=True)

D. np.unique(my_array, return_freq=True)

Answer: C

Question 3:

Which of the following functions can be used to load a CSV file into a NumPy array?

A. genfromtxt()

B. loadtxt()

C. loadtxt()

D. genfromcsv()

Answer: A

Exercise 4.2

Generate a NumPy array of shape 5 x 7 containing random integers between 1 and 50. Find the mean, median, minimum, and maximum values across columns and rows.

Solution:

```
importnumpyasnp
my_array = np.random.randint(1,50, size = (5,7))

print("Original")
print(my_array)

print("mean:")
print(np.mean(my_array, axis = 1))
print(np.mean(my_array, axis = 0))

print("median:")
print(np.median(my_array, axis = 1))
print(np.median(my_array, axis = 0))

print("min:")
print(np.amin(my_array, axis = 1))
print(np.amin(my_array, axis = 0))

print("max:")
print(np.amax(my_array, axis = 1))
print(np.amax(my_array, axis = 0))
```

Exercise 5.1

Question 1:

How to find the dot product between two numpy arrays, A and B?

A. numpy.dot(A,B)

B. A.dot(B)

C. Both A and B

D. None of the above

Answer: C

Question 2:

How to find the determinant of a Matrix A?

A. numpy.linalg.det(A)

B. numpy.det(A)

C. linalg.det(A)

D. All of the above

Answer: A

Question 3:

How to find the sine of an item in a NumPy array?

A. numpy.sine()

B. numpy.sin()

C. numpy.linalg.sin()

D. None of the above

Answer: B

Exercise 5.2

Solve the following system of of three linear equations and find the values of variables x, y, and z:

```
3x + 4y + 2z = 17

5x + 2y + 3z = 23

4x + 3y + 2z = 19
```

Solution:

```
importnumpyasnp

A = np.array([[3, 4, 2],
       [5, 2, 3],
       [4, 3, 2]])

B = np.array([17, 23, 19])


X = np.linalg.inv(A).dot(B)
print(X)
```

Exercise 6.1

Question 1:

In a neural network with three input features, one hidden layer of five nodes, and an output layer with three possible values, what will be the dimensions of weight that connect the input to the hidden layer? Remember, the dimensions of the input data are (m,3), where m is the number of records.

A. [5,3]

B. [3,5]

C. [4,5]

D. [5,4]

Answer: B

Question 2:

Which activation function do you use in the output layer in case of multiclass classification problems?

A. Sigmoid

B. Negative log likelihood

C. Relu

D. Softmax

Answer: D

Question 3:

Neural networks with hidden layers are capable of finding:

A. Linear Boundaries

B. Non-linear Boundaries

C. All of the above

D. None of the Above

Answer: C

Exercise 6.2

Try to classify the following dataset with three classes by implementing a multiclass classification neural network from scratch using the NumPy library in Python:

```
importnumpyasnp
importmatplotlib.pyplotasplt

np.random.seed(42)

cat1 = np.random.randn(800, 2) + np.array([0, -2])
cat2 = np.random.randn(800, 2) + np.array([2, 2])
cat3 = np.random.randn(800, 2) + np.array([-3, -3])

X = np.vstack([cat1, cat2, cat3])

labels = np.array([0]*800 + [1]*800 + [2]*800)

y = np.zeros((2400, 3))

foriinrange(2400):
y[i, labels[i]] = 1

x1 = X[:,0]
x2 = X[:,1]

plt.figure(figsize=(10,7))
plt.scatter(x1, x2, c= y, cmap=plt.cm.coolwarm)
```

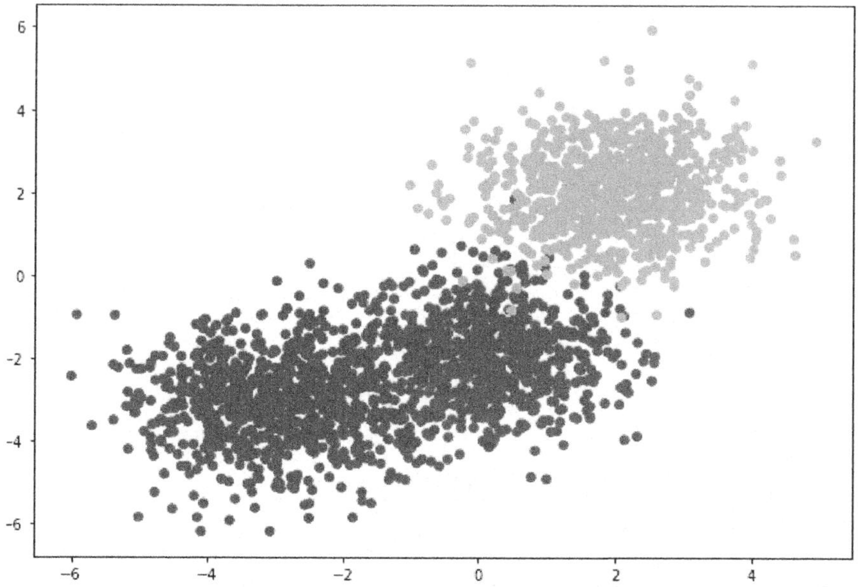

Solution:

```
defdefine_parameters(weights):
weight_list = []
bias_list = []
foriinrange(len(weights) - 1):

    w = np.random.randn(weights[i], weights[i+1])
    b = np.random.randn()

weight_list.append(w)
bias_list.append(b)

returnweight_list, bias_list

defsoftmax(X):
expX = np.exp(X)
returnexpX / expX.sum(axis=1, keepdims=True)

defsigmoid(x):
return1/(1+np.exp(-x))


defsigmoid_der(x):
return sigmoid(x)*(1-sigmoid(x))


defpredictions(w, b, X):
zh = np.dot(X,w[0]) + b[0]
  ah = sigmoid(zh)

  zo = np.dot(ah, w[1]) + b[1]
ao = softmax(zo)
returnao


deffind_cost(ao,y):

total_cost = np.sum(-y * np.log(ao))
returntotal_cost
```

```
deffind_derivatives(w, b, X):

zh = np.dot(X,w[0]) + b[0]
  ah = sigmoid(zh)

  zo = np.dot(ah, w[1]) + b[1]
ao = softmax(zo)

# Backpropagation phase 1


dcost_dzo = (ao-y)
dzo_dwo = ah.T

dwo= np.dot(dzo_dwo, dcost_dzo)
dbo = np.sum(dcost_dzo)

# Backpropagation phase 2

# dcost_wh = dcost_dah * dah_dzh * dzh_dwh
# dcost_dah = dcost_dzo * dzo_dah


dzo_dah = w[1].T

dcost_dah = np.dot(dcost_dzo , dzo_dah)

dah_dzh = sigmoid_der(zh)
dzh_dwh = X.T
dwh = np.dot(dzh_dwh, dah_dzh * dcost_dah)
dbh = np.sum(dah_dzh * dcost_dah)

returndwh, dbh, dwo, dbo

defupdate_weights(w,b,dwh, dbh, dwo, dbo, lr):
w[0] = w[0] - lr * dwh
w[1] = w[1] - lr * dwo
```

```
b[0] = b[0] - lr * dbh
b[1] = b[1] - lr * dbo

return w, b

defmy_multiout_neural_network(X, y, lr, epochs):
error_list = []
input_len = X.shape[1]
output_len = y.shape[1]
w,b = define_parameters([input_len, 10, output_len])

foriinrange(epochs):
ao = predictions(w, b, X)
    cost = find_cost(ao, y)
error_list.append(cost)
dwh, dbh, dwo, dbo = find_derivatives (w, b, X)
    w, b = update_weights(w, b, dwh, dbh, dwo, dbo, lr )
ifi % 50 == 0 :
print(cost)

return w, b, error_list



lr = 0.005
epochs = 1000
w, b, error_list = my_multiout_neural_network(X,y,lr,epochs)
```

From the Same Publisher

Python Machine Learning

https://bit.ly/3gcb2iG

Python Deep Learning

https://bit.ly/3gci9Ys

Python Data Visualization

https://bit.ly/3wXqDJI

Python for Data Analysis

https://bit.ly/3wPYEM2

Python Data Preprocessing

https://bit.ly/3fLV3ci

Python for NLP

https://bit.ly/3chlTqm

10 ML Projects Explained from Scratch

https://bit.ly/34KFsDk

Python Scikit-Learn for Beginners

https://bit.ly/3fPbtRf

Made in the USA
Monee, IL
05 November 2026

67914365R00108